BRIEF CONTENTS

Johonnes michael
Temesgen_go.ta5

Configuring Windows 8®
Exam 70-687

Lab Manual

Craig Zacker
Patrick Regan

WILEY

EXECUTIVE EDITOR	John Kane
EDITORIAL ASSISTANT	Allison Winkle
DIRECTOR OF SALES	Mitchell Beaton
EXECUTIVE MARKETING MANAGER	Chris Ruel
SENIOR PRODUCTION & MANUFACTURING MANAGER	Janis Soo
ASSOCIATE PRODUCTION MANAGER	Joel Balbin
PRODUCTION EDITOR	Eugenia Lee

www.wiley.com/college/microsoft or
call the MOAC Toll-Free Number: 888-764-7001 (U.S. & Canada only)

ISBN 978-1-118-55080-9

Printed in the United States of America

10 9 8 7 6 5 4 3 2 1

CONTENTS

LAB 1 EVALUATING HARDWARE READINESS AND CAPABILITY

THIS LAB CONTAINS THE FOLLOWING EXERCISES AND ACTIVITIES:

Exercise 1.1	Evaluating Your Machine
Exercise 1.2	Running the Upgrade Assistant
Lab Challenge	Reviewing Your Upgrade Options

BEFORE YOU BEGIN

The lab environment consists of student workstations connected to a local area network, along with a server that functions as the domain controller for a domain called adatum.com. The computers required for this lab are listed in Table 1-1.

Table 1-1
Computers Required for Lab 1

Computer	*Operating System*	*Computer Name*
Server	Windows Server 2012	SVR-DC-A
Client	Windows 7 Enterprise	WKSTN-MBR-D

In addition to the computers, you will also need the software listed in Table 1-2 to complete Lab 1.

Table 1-2
Software Required for Lab 1

Software	***Location***
Windows 8 Upgrade Assistant (Windows8-UpgradeAssistant.exe)	\\SVR-DC-A\software
Lab 1 student worksheet	Lab01_worksheet.docx (provided by instructor)

Working with Lab Worksheets

Each lab in this manual requires that you answer questions, shoot screen shots, and perform other activities that you will document in a worksheet named for the lab, such as Lab01_worksheet.docx. You will find these worksheets on the book companion site. It is recommended that you use a USB flash drive to store your worksheets so you can submit them to your instructor for review. As you perform the exercises in each lab, open the appropriate worksheet file, type the required information, and then save the file to your flash drive.

SCENARIO

After completing this lab, you will be able to:

- Use basic tools to evaluate your PC's hardware
- Run the Upgrade Assistant to determine if your machine can be upgraded to Windows 8

Estimated lab time: 35 minutes

Exercise 1.1	Evaluating Your Machine
Overview	In this exercise, you will use several built-in tools to view the current Windows version and hardware.
Mindset	Before you install or deploy Windows to a machine, you need identify what hardware the machine has and if that hardware meets the minimum requirements for Windows 8. An enterprise organization may have a software component that can perform inventory. However, you must still identify the hardware of a computer using the built-in tools that are included with Windows 8.
Completion time	10 minutes

1. On **WKSTN-MBR-D**, log on using the **adatum\administrator** account and the **Pa$$w0rd** password.
2. Click **Start**, then right-click **Computer** and choose **Properties**.

Question 1	*What version and edition of Windows are you using? Is it a 32-bit or 64-bit version of Windows*

Question 2	*How much memory does your system have?*

3. Close the *System* window.

4. Click the **Start** > **All Programs** > **Accessories** > **System Tools** > **System Information** (see Figure 1-1).

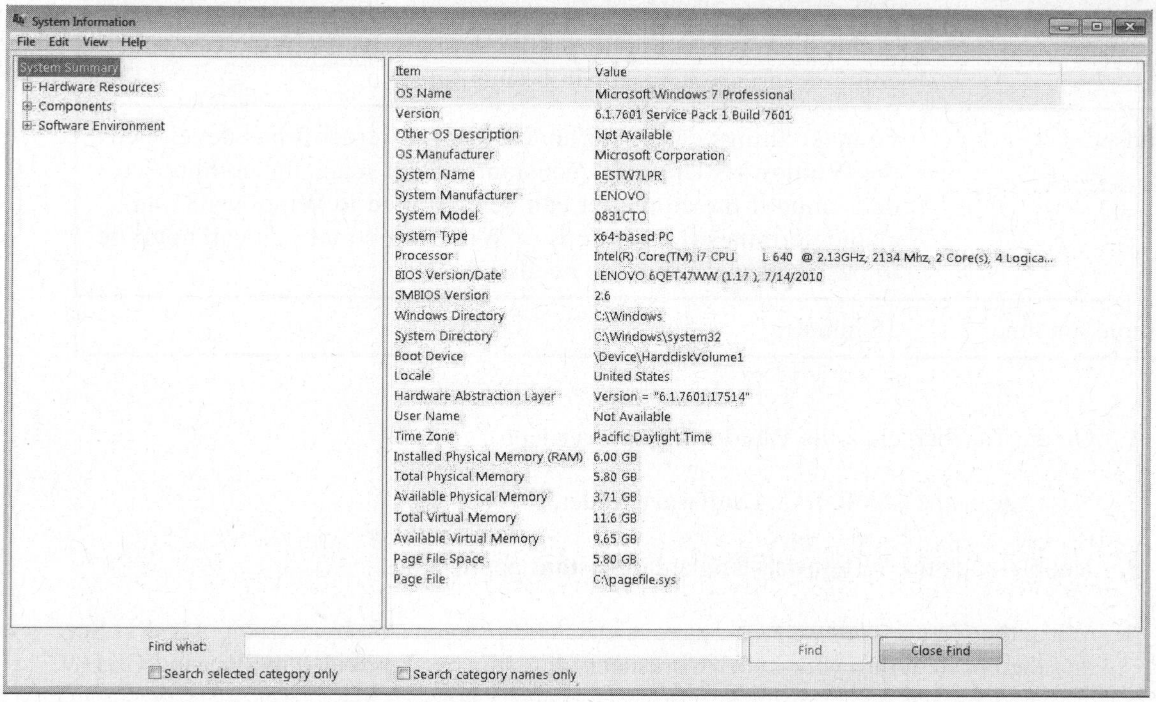

Figure 1-1
The System Information window

Question 3	*Which version are you using?*

Question 4	*Which processor or processors do you have?*

5. Close the *System Information* window.

6. On the Taskbar, click the **Windows Explorer** icon.

7. Click **Computer**.

Question 5	*How much disk space do you have on your C drive?*

End of exercise. Leave the computer logged into WKSTN-MBR-C for the next exercise.

Exercise 1.2	Running the Upgrade Assistant
Overview	In this exercise, you will run the upgrade assistant to scan your computer to see what it can be upgraded to.
Mindset	To make things easier for an end-user, Microsoft has developed the Windows 8 Upgrade Assistant, which scans the computer to determine if the computer can be upgraded to Windows 8 and also determines the versions of Windows 8 that you can upgrade to based on your upgrade needs.
Completion time	15 minutes

1. On the Taskbar, click the **Windows Explorer** icon.

2. Navigate to the **\\SVR-DC-A\software** folder.

3. Double-click the **Windows8-UpgradeAssistant** application.

4. When the *Here's what we found* page opens, take a screen shot by pressing **Alt+Prt Scr** and then paste it into your Lab 1 worksheet file in the page provided by pressing **Ctrl+V**.

5. Click **See compatibility details**.

Question 6	*Which items do you need to review?*

6. Click **Close**.

7. Click **Next**.

8. Log off of **WKSTN-MBR-C**.

Lab Challenge	Review Your Upgrade options
Overview	During this exercise, you will perform a written exercise to ensure that you understand the available installation and upgrade options.
Mindset	Prior to installing or deploying Windows, you must look at the hardware that you want to use and determine if the computer can handle Windows 8. If the hardware cannot, you will need to determine if you want to upgrade the current hardware, or replace the computer.
Completion time	10 minutes

For this written exercise, answer the following questions based on the given scenario.

1. You are visiting a client that has a computer running Windows 7. However, you do not know the specifications for the computer. What tool or option can you use to quickly view the computer name, domain name, processor information, installed memory, if the system is 32-bit or 64-bit, the edition of Windows, and if Windows 7 includes a service pack or not?

2. You are purchasing a computer with Windows 8. You need to be able to add the computer to an Active Directory Domain. You will need to be able to access shared folders and printers on the network, and you need to share your printer to other users. You will need to be able to run a virtual machine running Windows XP on the computer. You will also need to install Office 2013. What is the least expensive edition of Windows 8 that you will need?

3. What is the maximum number of processors that Windows 8 Professional can support?

4. You have a computer that has a Intel quad-core processor. Can you run Windows 8 Professional and will Windows be able to use all four cores?

5. You have an application that will require 8 GB of memory. What is the least expensive edition and version of Windows 8 that you can use for this application to run?

6. You want Windows 8 to use BranchCache. What is the least expensive edition of Windows 8 that you can use?

7. You have a computer running Windows 7 Professional. Which version of Windows can you perform an in-place upgrade to?

8. You have Windows Vista. You want to upgrade to Windows 8 while keeping all of the applications. How should you upgrade the system?

End of lab.

LAB 2
INSTALLING WINDOWS 8

THIS LAB CONTAINS THE FOLLOWING EXERCISES AND ACTIVITIES:

Exercise 2.1 Performing a Clean Windows 8 Installation

Exercise 2.2 Joining a Domain

Lab Challenge Upgrading Windows 7 to Windows 8

BEFORE YOU BEGIN

The lab environment consists of computers connected to a local area network. The computers required for this lab are listed in Table 2-1.

Table 2-1
Computers Required for Lab 2

Computer	*Operating System*	*Computer Name*
Server	Windows Server 2012	SVR-DC-A
New workstation	Bare Metal	WKSTN-MBR-B
Workstation for upgrade	Windows 7 Enterprise	WKSTN-MBR-D

In addition to the computers, you will also need the software listed in Table 2-2 to complete Lab 2.

Table 2-2
Software Required for Lab 2

Software	*Location*
Installation disk for Windows 8 Enterprise	Mounted on WKSTN-MBR-B
Installation disk for Windows 8 Enterprise	Mounted on WKSTN-MBR-D
Lab 2 student worksheet	Lab02_worksheet.docx (provided by instructor)

Working with Lab Worksheets

Each lab in this manual requires that you answer questions, create screenshots, and perform other activities that you will document in a worksheet named for the lab, such as Lab02_worksheet.docx. You will find these worksheets on the book companion site. It is recommended that you use a USB flash drive to store your worksheets so you can submit them to your instructor for review. As you perform the exercises in each lab, open the appropriate worksheet file, type the required information, and then save the file to your flash drive.

SCENARIO

After completing this lab, you will be able to:

- Perform a clean Windows 8 installation on a bare metal computer
- Join a Windows 8 workstation to an Active Directory Domain Services domain
- Upgrade a Windows 7 workstation to Windows 8

Estimated lab time: 60 minutes

Exercise 2.1	Performing a Clean Windows 8 Installation
Overview	In this exercise, you will install Windows 8 on a new computer that has no previously installed operating system.
Mindset	In many cases, organizations purchase computers without operating systems installed—sometimes called bare metal workstations—either because they have an existing license agreement or because they intend to purchase the operating system (OS) through a different channel. In these cases, you perform what is known as a clean operating system installation, which is a procedure that creates a new server with the default operating system settings.
Completion time	30 minutes

1. Select the **WKSTN-MBR-B** computer, on which the Windows 8 installation disk is mounted and loaded. The *Windows Setup* page appears.

2. Accept the default values for the *Language to install* setting, the *Time and currency format* setting, and the *Keyboard or input method* setting by clicking **Next**. Another *Windows Setup* page appears.

3. Click the **Install now** button. The *License terms* page appears.

4. Select *I accept the license terms* and then click **Next**. The *Which type of installation do you want?* page appears.

5. Click **Custom: Install Windows only (advanced)**. The *Where do you want to install Windows?* page appears (see Figure 2-1).

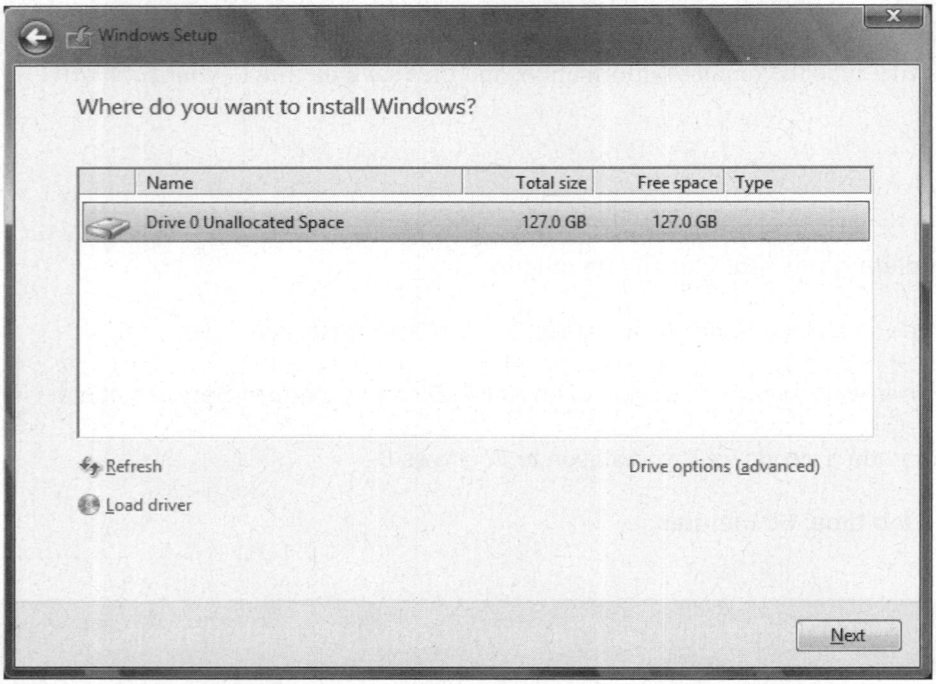

Figure 2-1
The *Where do you want to install Windows?* page

6. Leave **Drive 0 Unallocated Space** selected and then click **Next**. The *Installing Windows* page appears as the system installs Windows 8.

Question 1	*What should you do if the drive on which you want to install Windows 8 already has a partition on it containing an operating system and data you do not need?*

Question 2	*What should you do if the* Where do you want to install Windows? *page appears, but it does not list any drives or partitions?*

7. After several minutes and a system restart, the *Personalize* page appears.

8. In the *PC name* textbox, type **WKSTN-MBR-B** and then click **Next**. The *Settings* page appears.

9. Click **Use express settings**. The *Sign in to your PC* page appears.

10. Click **Sign in without a Microsoft account**. Another *Sign in to your PC page* appears.

11. Click **Local account**. The next *Sign in to your PC page* appears (see Figure 2-2).

12. Take a screen shot of the *Sign in to your PC page* by pressing **Alt+Prt Scr** and then paste it into your Lab 2 worksheet file in the page provided by pressing **Ctrl+V**.

13. In the *User name* text box, type **ocox**. In the *Password* text box and in the *Reenter password* text box, type **Pa$$w0rd**. In the *Password hint* text box, type **ocox** and then click Finish. After a brief introduction to Windows 8, the Start screen appears.

End of exercise. Leave all windows open for the next exercise.

Exercise 2.2	Joining a Domain
Overview	In this exercise, you will join your newly installed Windows 8 workstation to your network's Active Directory Domain Services domain.
Mindset	To function in an enterprise environment, Windows 8 workstations typically must be part of an Active Directory domain. An administrator must join the workstation to the domain by supplying appropriate credentials.
Completion time	10 minutes

1. Click the **Desktop** tile, mouse over the lower-left corner of the desktop and then right-click the **Start** screen thumbnail that appears there. Then, from the context menu that appears, click **Control Panel**. The *Control Panel* window appears.

2. Click **Network** and **Internet** > **Network and Sharing Center**. The *Network and Sharing Center* window appears.

3. Click **Change adapter settings**. The *Network Connections* window appears.

4. Right-click the **Ethernet** connection and choose **Properties**. The *Ethernet Properties* sheet appears.

5. Double-click **Internet Protocol Version 4 (TCP/IPv4)**. The *Internet Protocol Version 4 (TCP/IPv4) Properties* sheet appears.

6. Select the **Use the following IP address** option and then type values in the following text boxes:

   - *IP address:* **10.0.0.2**
   - *Subnet mask:* **255.255.255.0**

7. Select the **Use the following DNS server addresses** option and then type a value in the following text box:

   - *Preferred DNS server:* **10.0.0.1**

8. Click **OK** to close the *Internet Protocol Version 4 (TCP/IPv4) Properties* sheet.

9. Click **OK** to close the *Ethernet Properties* sheet.

10. Close the *Network Connections* window. Click the Control Panel Home link in the left pane.

11. In *Control Panel*, click **System and Security > System**. The *System* control panel appears.

12. Click **Change settings**. The *System Properties* sheet appears.

13. Click **Change**. The *Computer Name/Domain Changes* dialog box appears (see Figure 2-2).

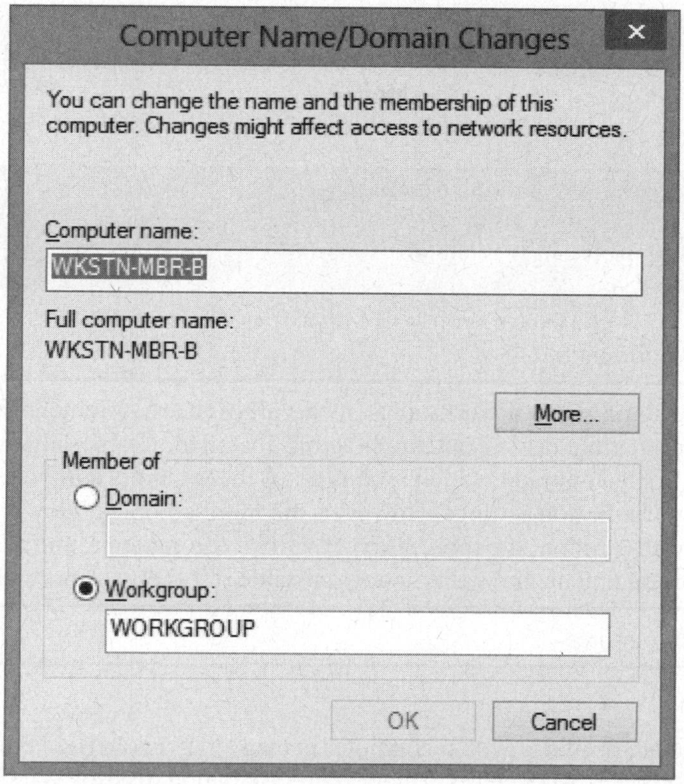

Figure 2-2
The *Computer Name/Domain Changes* dialog box

14. Select the **Domain** option, type **adatum.com** in the text box, and then click **OK**. A *Windows Security* dialog box appears.

Question 3	*What is the primary reason for the joining to a domain to fail at this point?*

15. Authenticate with a *User name* of **Administrator** and a *Password* of **Pa$$w0rd** and then click **OK**. A message box appears, welcoming you to the domain.

16. Take a screen shot of the message box by pressing **Alt+Prt Scr** and then paste it into your Lab 2 worksheet file in the page provided by pressing **Ctrl+V**.

17. Click **OK**. Another message box appears, prompting you to restart the computer.

18. Click **OK**.

19. Click **Close** to close the *System Properties* dialog box.

20. A *You must restart your computer to apply these changes* message box appears.

21. Click **Restart Now**. The computer restarts.

End of exercise.

Lab Challenge	Upgrading Windows 7 to Windows 8
Overview	In this challenge, you will upgrade a Windows 7 workstation to Windows 8.
Mindset	Assuming that a workstation meets all of the requirements and has compatible drivers and applications installed, it is possible to perform an in-place upgrade, which retains all of the system's software, data, and configuration settings. However, the more complex the workstation configuration, the more likely it will be for incompatibilities to arise, producing an end result that is unstable or otherwise problematic.
Completion time	20 minutes

In this challenge, you are provided with a computer named WKSTN-MBR-D that is running Windows 7. In the computer's DVD drive, there is an installation disk for Windows 8 Enterprise, which you must use to upgrade the operating system from Windows 7 to Windows 8. To complete the challenge, complete the following tasks:

1. Windows 7, as configured on WKSTN-MBR-D, is running Internet Information Services. Before you begin the upgrade process, demonstrate that IIS is running by taking a screen shot of the IIS default website. Press **Alt+Prt Scr** and then paste it into your Lab 2 worksheet file in the page provided by pressing **Ctrl+V**.

2. Upgrade the workstation to Windows 8, documenting the process by listing the basic steps you performed.

Note	*The length of time required for the Windows 8 upgrade process can be 20 minutes or more, depending on the number and type of applications, files, and configuration settings on the computer at the outset.*

3. Demonstrate that IIS is still running on the upgraded workstation by taking a screen shot of the new IIS default website. Press **Alt+Prt Scr** and then paste it into your Lab 2 worksheet file in the page provided by pressing **Ctrl+V**.

4. Answer the following questions:

a. Under what conditions would the Upgrade option be unavailable to you during the Windows 8 installation process?

b. The compatibility notes that appear during this exercise are recommendations; they do not prevent you from performing the upgrade. However, in a real-world upgrade situation, this might not be the case. Give an example of a compatibility note that will stop the upgrade process and force you to take action before restarting the installation.

End of lab.

LAB 3
MIGRATING AND CONFIGURING USER DATA

THIS LAB CONTAINS THE FOLLOWING EXERCISES AND ACTIVITIES:

Exercise 3.1 Collecting User Profile Data

Exercise 3.2 Importing User Profile Data

Lab Challenge Migrating User Profiles Over the Network

BEFORE YOU BEGIN

The lab environment consists of computers connected to a local area network. The computers required for this lab are listed in Table 3-1.

Table 3-1
Computers Required for Lab 3

Computer	***Operating System***	***Computer Name***
Server	Windows Server 2012	SVR-DC-A
Workstation	Windows 8 Enterprise	WKSTN-MBR-B
Workstation	Windows 7 Enterprise	WKSTN-MBR-C

In addition to the computers, you will also require the software listed in Table 3-2 to complete Lab 3.

Table 3-2
Software Required for Lab 3

Software	*Location*
Lab 3 student worksheet	Lab03_worksheet.docx (provided by instructor)

Working with Lab Worksheets

Each lab in this manual requires that you answer questions, create screenshots, and perform other activities that you will document in a worksheet named for the lab, such as Lab03_worksheet.docx. You will find these worksheets on the book companion site. It is recommended that you use a USB flash drive to store your worksheets so you can submit them to your instructor for review. As you perform the exercises in each lab, open the appropriate worksheet file, type the required information, and then save the file to your flash drive.

SCENARIO

After completing this lab, you will be able to:

- Collect user profile data using Windows Easy Transfer
- Import user profile data
- Migrate user profiles over the network

Estimated lab time: 60 minutes

Exercise 3.1	Collecting User Profile Data
Overview	In this exercise, you will create users on a Windows 7 workstation and then run the Windows Easy Transfer program to collect the user profile data that you will migrate to Windows 8.
Mindset	Windows Easy Transfer enables you to save user profile data to a file on a network share or a removable medium and then import it to another computer. You can use this method to perform either a side-by-side migration or a wipe-and-load migration.
Completion time	20 minutes

1. On **WKSTN-MBR-C**, log in as local user Admin with the Pa$$w0rd password and then click **Start** > **Control Panel** > **System and Security** > **Administrative Tools**. The *Administrative Tools* control panel appears.

2. Double-click **Computer Management**. The *Computer Management* console appears.

3. Expand the **Local Users and Groups** node and then click the **Users** container.

4. Right-click the **Users** container and, from the context menu, click **New User**. The *New User* dialog box appears.

5. In the *User Name* text box, type **Alice**. In the *Password* text box and the *Confirm password* text box, type **Pa$$w0rd**.

6. Clear the **User must change password at next logon** check box and then click **Create**. The system creates the user account and then presents a blank new *User* dialog box.

7. Repeat steps 5 and 6 to create three additional user accounts named **Ralph**, **Ed**, and **Trixie**.

8. Click **Close**. The four new accounts appear in the *Users* container.

9. Click the Start icon and in the **Shut down** menu, click **Log off**.

10. Log on using the –.**\Alice** account you just created and the **Pa$$w0rd** password.

11. Repeat the previous two steps to log off and log on again, first using the **Ralph** account and then using the **Ed** account (using **Pa$$w0rd** as the password).

12. Log off the workstation.

13. Log on using the **adatum\Administrator** account and the **Pa$$w0rd** password.

14. Click **Start**. In the *Search programs and files* text box, type **Windows Easy Transfer** and then press **Enter**.

15. The *Windows Easy Transfer Wizard* appears, displaying the *Welcome to Windows Easy Transfer* page.

16. Click **Next**. The *What do you want to use to transfer items to your new computer?* page appears.

17. Click **An external hard disk or USB flash drive**. The *Which computer are you using now?* page appears.

18. Click **This is my old computer**. The program scans the computer for files and settings it can transfer and then displays the results in the *Choose what to transfer from this computer* page (see Figure 3-1).

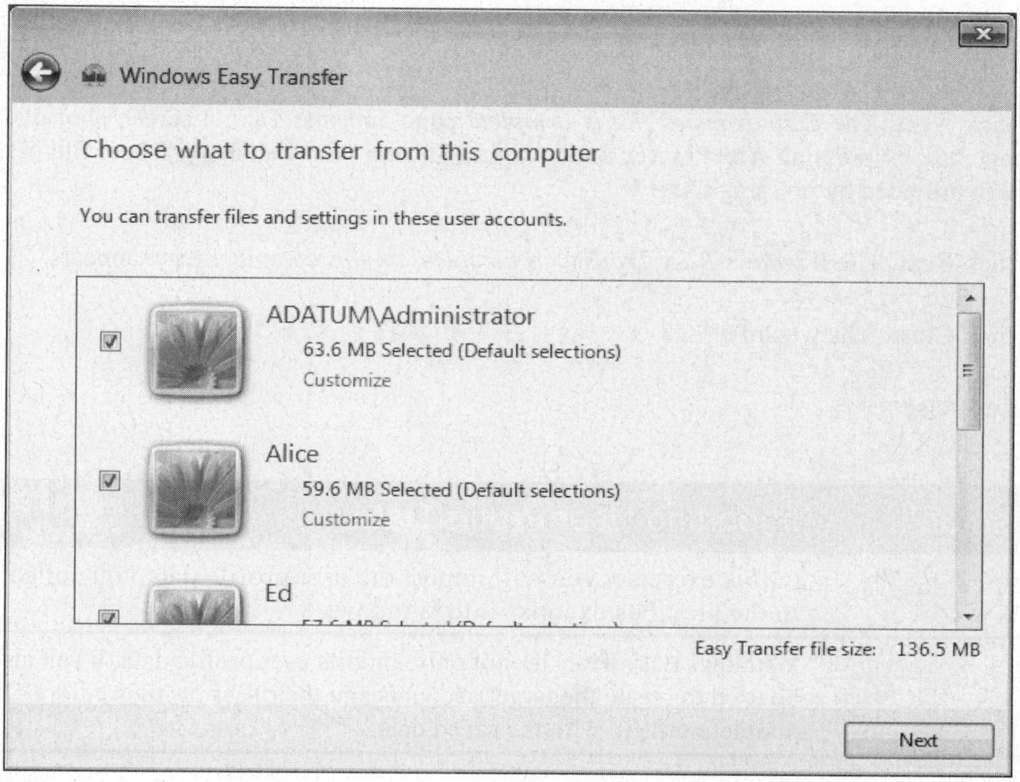

Figure 3-1
The *Choose what to transfer from this computer* page

Question 1	*Of the four users you created in this exercise, which have user profiles that are available for transfer?*

19. Leave the checkboxes selected for all of the available accounts as well as the *Shared Items* object and then click **Next**. The *Save your files and settings for transfer* page appears.

Question 2	*Why aren't the user profiles for all of the accounts you created available for transfer?*

20. In the *Password* text box and the *Confirm Password* text box, type **Pa$$w0rd** and then click **Save**. The *Save your Easy Transfer file* combo box appears.

21. In the *File Name* text box, type **\\svr-dc-a\downloads\Windows Easy Transfer - Items from old computer** and then click **Save**. The wizard saves the selected profiles to the lab server and then displays a *These files and settings have been saved for your transfer* page.

22. Click **Next**. The *Your transfer file is complete* page appears. Take a screen shot of the page box by pressing **Alt+Prt Scr** and then paste it into your Lab 3 worksheet file in the page provided by pressing **Ctrl+V**.

23. Click **Next**. The *Windows Easy Transfer is complete on this computer* page appears.

24. Click **Close**. The wizard closes.

End of exercise.

Exercise 3.2	Importing User Profile Data
Overview	In this exercise, you will import the user profile data you collected in the previous exercise into Windows 8.
Mindset	Windows Easy Transfer not only imports user profile data, it can also be used to create the target accounts and their user profiles before populating them with the saved data.
Completion time	20 minutes

1. On **WKSTN-MBR-B**, log on using the **adatum\Administrator** account and the **Pa$$w0rd** password.

2. At the *Start* screen, type **Windows Easy Transfer**. The *Apps Results* screen appears.

3. Click **Windows Easy Transfer**. The *Windows Easy Transfer Wizard* appears, displaying the *Welcome to Windows Easy Transfer* page.

4. Click **Next**. The *What do you want to use to transfer items to your new computer?* page appears.

5. Click *An external hard disk or USB flash drive*. The *Which PC are you using now?* page appears.

6. Click **This is my new PC**. The *Has Windows Easy Transfer already saved your files from your old computer to an external hard disk or USB flash drive?* page appears.

7. Click **Yes**. The *Open an Easy Transfer file* combo box appears.

8. In the *File Name* text box, type **\\svr-dc-a\downloads\Windows Easy Transfer - Items from old computer** and then click **Open**. The *Enter the password you used to help protect your transfer file and start the transfer* page appears.

9. In the text box, type **Pa$$w0rd** and then click **Next**. The wizard opens the file and then displays the *Choose what to transfer to this PC* page (see Figure 3-2).

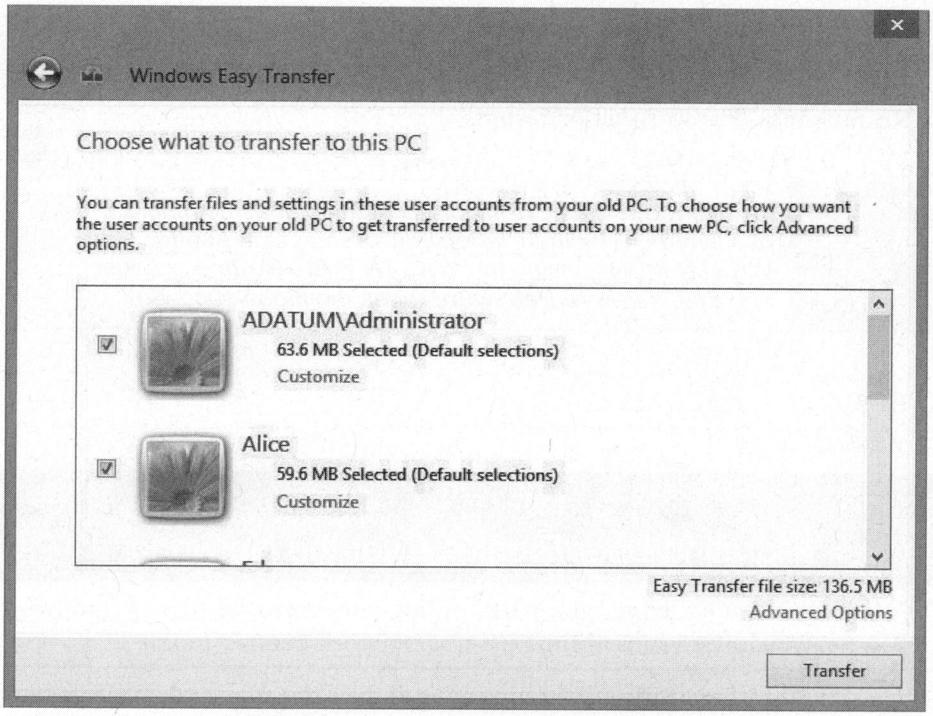

Figure 3-2
The *Choose what to transfer to this PC* page

10. Select all of the available items and then click **Advanced Options**. The *Advanced Options* dialog box appears.

11. For the **Alice** user account, select **Create User** in the appropriate drop-down menu. The *Create New User* dialog box appears.

12. In the *User Name* text box, type **Alice**. In the *Password* text box and the *Confirm password* text box, type **Pas$$w0rd** and then click **Create**.

13. Repeat steps 11 and 12 for the **Ed** user account and the **Ralph** user account. Click **Save**.

14. Click **Transfer**. The wizard transfers the settings you saved from the Windows 7 workstation to your Windows 8 workstation and then displays the *Your transfer is complete* page.

15. Click **See what was transferred**. The *Windows Easy Transfer Reports* window appears.

16. Take a screen shot of the *Windows Easy Transfer Reports* window by pressing **Alt+Prt Scr** and then paste it into your Lab 3 worksheet file in the page provided by pressing **Ctrl+V**.

17. Close the *Windows Easy Transfer Reports* window.

18. Click **Close**. A *Restart your PC to complete your transfer* dialog box appears.

19. Click **Restart now**. The workstation restarts.

Question 3	*The Windows Easy Transfer application does not migrate passwords. Why then, when you attempt to log on to WKSTN-MBR-B using the* ***WKSTN-MBR-B\Alice*** *account and the password* ***Pa$$w0rd****, does the logon succeed?*

End of exercise.

Lab Challenge	Migrating User Profiles Over the Network
Overview	In this challenge, you will migrate a user profile from Windows 7 to Windows 8 in real time using a network connection.
Mindset	When two workstations are active at the same time and connected to the same network, you can use Windows Easy Transfer to migrate user profiles directly between them without having to save the profile information to a file.
Completion time	20 minutes

A user wants to transfer user profiles from a Windows 7 workstation to a Windows 8 workstation, but these two computers are connected to the network at the same time. To complete this challenge, you must create a user profile for the Trixie account you created on WKSTN-MBR-C and transfer it directly to the WKSTN-MBR-B workstation using the network. Then complete the following tasks:

1. Write out the steps you performed to complete the challenge.

2. Take a screen shot of the *Go to your new computer and enter your Windows Easy Transfer key* page on the Windows 7 workstation by pressing **Alt+Prt Scr** and then paste it into your Lab 3 worksheet file in the page provided by pressing **Ctrl+V**.

3. Take a screen shot of the *Enter your Windows Easy Transfer key* page on the Windows 8 workstation by pressing **Alt+Prt Scr** and then paste it into your Lab 3 worksheet file in the page provided by pressing **Ctrl+V**.

End of lab.

LAB 4
CONFIGURING DEVICES AND DEVICE DRIVERS

THIS LAB CONTAINS THE FOLLOWING EXERCISES AND ACTIVITIES:

BEFORE YOU BEGIN

The lab environment consists of student workstations connected to a local area network, along with a server that functions as the domain controller for a domain called adatum.com. The computers required for this lab are listed in Table 4-1.

Table 4-1
Computers Required for Lab 4

Computer	*Operating System*	*Computer Name*
Server	Windows Server 2012	SVR-DC-A
Client	Windows 8 Enterprise	WKSTN-MBR-B

In addition to the computers, you will also need the software listed in Table 4-2 to complete Lab 4.

Table 4-2
Software required for Lab 4

Software	*Location*
Lab 4 student worksheet	Lab04_worksheet.docx (provided by instructor)

Working with Lab Worksheets

Each lab in this manual requires that you answer questions, shoot screen shots, and perform other activities that you will document in a worksheet named for the lab, such as Lab04_worksheet.docx. You will find these worksheets on the book companion site. It is recommended that you use a USB flash drive to store your worksheets so you can submit them to your instructor for review. As you perform the exercises in each lab, open the appropriate worksheet file, fill in the required information, and then save the file to your flash drive.

SCENARIO

After completing this lab, you will be able to:

- View and manage devices with Device Manager
- Update a driver with Device Manager
- Rollback a driver with Device Manager

Estimated lab time: 50 minutes

Exercise 4.1	Troubleshooting Devices with Device Manager
Overview	In this exercise, you will use Device Manager to troubleshoot problems with devices and device drivers.
Mindset	While a hardware problem can be a physical failure of the device, often the problem is caused by not having the proper device driver loaded. To view hardware that Windows sees, to view the drivers that are loaded for the hardware devices, and to manage the hardware devices and drivers, you would use Device Manager.
Completion time	20 minutes

1. On WKSTN-MBR-B, log on using the **adatum\Administrator** account and the **Pa$$w0rd** password. When the Start menu appears, click the Desktop tile.

2. Mouse over the lower-left corner of the desktop and right-click the **Start** screen thumbnail that appears there. Click **Device Manager**.

Question 1	*Are there any errors or unknown devices?*

3. Expand the **Ports (COM and LPT)** node (see Figure 4-1).

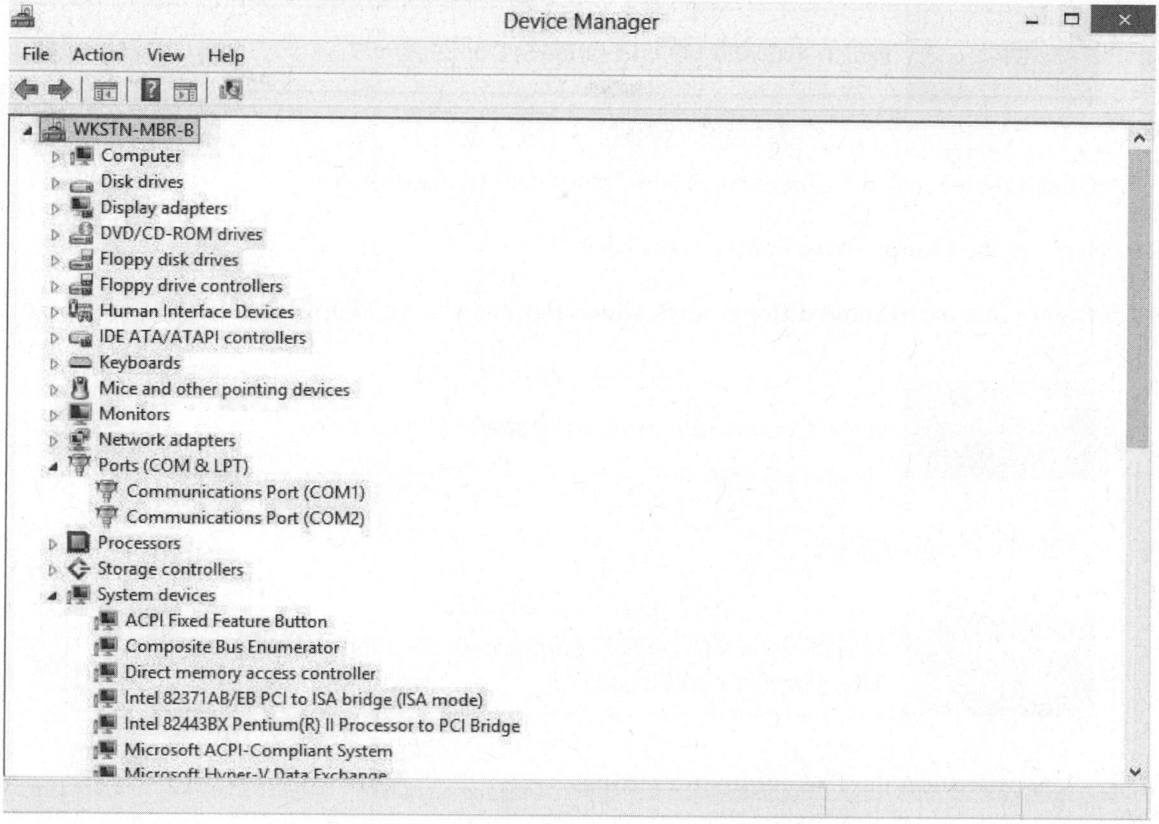

Figure 4-1
The Device Manager window

4. Right-click **Communications Port (COM2)** and choose **Disable**.

5. When you are prompted to confirm if you want to disable the device, click **Yes**.

Question 2	*Which icon represents a disabled device?*

6. Right-click the **Communications Port (COM2)** and choose **Enable**.

7. Right-click the **Communications Port (COM2)** and choose **Properties**.

Question 3	*In the General tab, what is the status of the device?*

8. Click the **Resources** tab.

Question 4	*Which IRQ and I/O port range is Com2 using?*

9. Click **OK** to close the *Communications Port (COM2)* dialog box.
10. Expand the **Floppy drive controllers** node.
11. Right-click the **Standard floppy disk controller** and choose **Properties**.

Question 5	*In the General tab, what is the status of the device?*

12. Click the **Resources** tab.

Question 6	*Which IRQ, DMA and I/O port ranges does the Standard floppy disk controller use?*

13. Click to deselect the **Use automatic settings**.

Note:	*Today, it would be extremely rare that you will ever have to manually configure these settings. This is for demonstration purposes only.*

14. Change *Setting based on* to **Basic configuration 0002**.
15. Double-click the **IRQ**. When the *Edit Interrupt Request* dialog box opens, change *Value* to **05**. Click **OK** to close the *Edit Interrupt Request* dialog box.
16. Click **OK** to close the *Standard floppy disk controller Properties* dialog box.
17. When you are prompted to confirm if you want to continue, click **Yes**.
18. When you are prompted to restart the computer, click **No**.

Question 7	*Which icon does the Standard floppy disk controller have now?*

19. Double-click **Standard floppy disk controller**.

Question 8	*What is the device status now?*

20. Click the Resources tab, take a screen shot of the *Resources* tab on the *Device Manager Standard floppy disk controller Properties* dialog box by pressing **Alt+Prt Scr** and then paste it into your Lab 4 worksheet file in the page provided by pressing **Ctrl+V**.

21. Click **Set Configuration Manually**.

22. Click to select **Use automatic settings**.

23. Click **OK** to close the *Standard floppy disk controller Properties* dialog box.

24. When you are prompted to restart the computer, click **Yes**.

End of exercise. Wait for WKSTN-MBR-B to reboot for the next exercise.

Exercise 4.2	Updating Device Drivers
Overview	In this exercise, you will update device drivers with Device Manager.
Mindset	There are multiple reasons why vendors may update a driver. They may need to fix an issue, allow the driver to run more efficiently, or additional capability or functionality. For whatever reason, you will update a driver.
Completion time	15 minutes

1. Log into **WKSTN-MBR-B** as **adatum\administrator** with the **Pa$$w0rd** password. When the Start menu opens, click the **Desktop** tile.

2. Mouse over the lower-left corner of the desktop and right-click the **Start** screen thumbnail that appears there. Click **Device Manager**.

3. Right-click **WKSTN-MBR-B** and choose **Scan for hardware changes**.

4. Expand the **Ports (COM and LPT)** node and then click **Communications Port (COM2) port**.

5. Right-click **Communications Port (COM2) port** and then click **Update Driver Software**.

6. When the *How do you want to search for driver software?* page opens, click **Search automatically for updated driver software**.

Question 9	*Which driver did it find and what does it say about the driver?*

7. Click **Close** to close the *Update Driver Software – Communications Port (COM2)* dialog box.

8. Right-click **Communications port (COM2)** and choose **Properties**.

9. Click the **Driver** tab (see Figure 4-2).

Figure 4-2
The *Driver* tab

Question 10	*Which driver version is Communication Port (COM2) using?*

10. Click **Update Driver**.

11. On the *How do you want to search for driver software?* page, click **Browse my computer for driver software**.

12. On the *Browse for driver software on your computer* page, click **Let me pick from a list of device drivers on my computer**.

13. On the *Select the device driver you want to install for this hardware* page, click to deselect the **Show compatible hardware**.

Note:	*Normally, you would not want to use other drivers that are not compatible. This is for demonstration purposes only.*

14. For the *Manufacturer* setting, click **Trimble** and then click **Trimble PCMICA GPS Adapter (Rev. B)**. Click **Next**.

15. When an update driver warning message appears, click **Yes**.

16. When the driver has been installed, click **Close.**

17. Take a screen shot of the *Trimble PMCIA GPS Adapter (Rev. B) (COM2) Properties* dialog box by pressing **Alt+Prt Scr** and then paste it into your Lab 4 worksheet file in the page provided by pressing **Ctrl+V**.

18. Click **Close** to close the *Trimble PCMCIA GPS Adapter (Rev. B) (COM2) Properties* dialog box.

End of exercise. Leave the Device Manager open for the next exercise.

Exercise 4.3	Rolling Back Drivers
Overview	In this exercise, you will use Device Manager to rollback a driver.
Mindset	From time to time, you will encounter problems when you upgrade a driver. So you will need to know how to roll back the driver.
Completion time	5 minutes

1. On **WKSTN-MBR-B**, using **Device Manager**, right-click the **Trimble PCMICA GPS Adapter (Rev B) (COM2)** and choose **Properties**.

2. Click the **Driver** tab (see Figure 4-3).

Figure 4-3
The *Driver* tab

3. Click **Roll Back Driver**.

4. When you are prompted to confirm if you would like to roll back to the previously installed driver software, click **Yes**.

5. Take a screen shot of the *Communications Port (COM2) Properties* dialog box by pressing **Alt+Prt Scr** and then paste it into your Lab 4 worksheet file in the page provided by pressing **Ctrl+V**.

6. Click **Close** to close the *Communications Port (COM2) Properties* dialog box.

End of exercise. You can close the Device Manager and leave the computer logged on for the lab challenge.

Lab Challenge	Accessing Advanced Boot Options
Overview	In this exercise, you will disable driver signature enforcement.
Mindset	On occasion, you may need to install a driver that you trust but has not been signed by the vendor. You can disable driver signature enforcement by modifying the Startup Settings.
Completion time	10 minutes

1. On **WKSTN-MBR-B**, mouse over the lower-right corner of the screen, and when the fly-out menu appears, click the **Settings** charm. The *Settings* menu appears.
2. Click **Change PC Settings**. The *PC Settings* menu appears.
3. Click **General**. The *General* menu appears.
4. Scroll down to the bottom. Under *Advanced Startup*, select **Restart Now**.
5. When the system restarts and the *Choose an option* page appears, click **Troubleshoot**. See Figure 4-4.

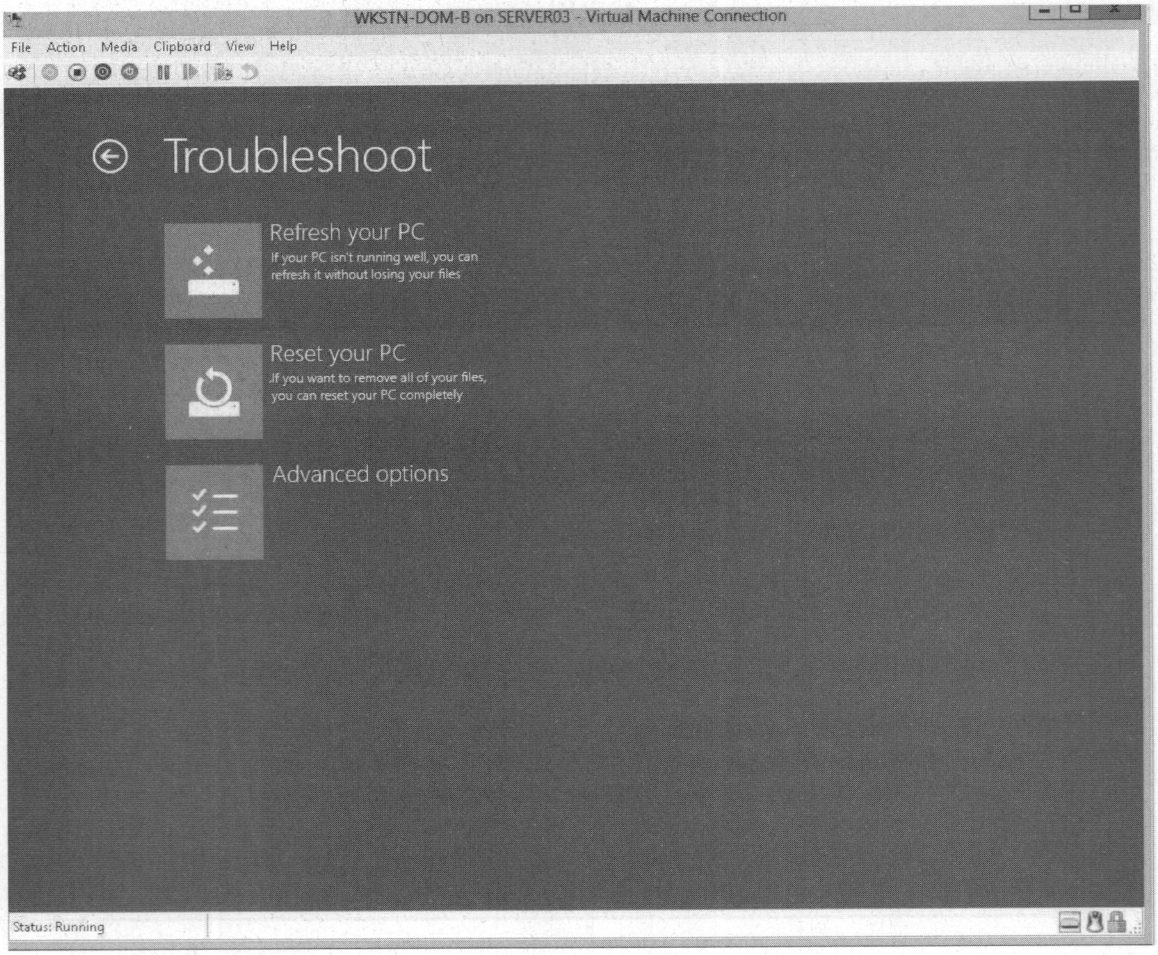

Figure 4-4
The Windows 8 Troubleshoot menu

6. On the *Troubleshoot* menu, click **Advanced Options**.
7. Click **Startup Settings**.
8. On the *Startup Settings* page, click **Restart**.
9. When the *Startup Settings* page appears, press **7** to disable driver signature enforcement. The system starts, loading all drivers, whether signed or not and whether altered or not.

End of lab.

LAB 5
INSTALLING AND CONFIGURING DESKTOP APPLICATIONS

THIS LAB CONTAINS THE FOLLOWING EXERCISES AND ACTIVITIES:

Exercise 5.1	Setting File Associations
Exercise 5.2	Setting Compatibility Modes
Lab Challenge	Modifying File Associations

BEFORE YOU BEGIN

The lab environment consists of computers connected to a local area network. The computers required for this lab are listed in Table 5-1.

Table 5-1
Computers Required for Lab 5

Computer	*Operating System*	*Computer Name*
Server	Windows Server 2012	SVR-DC-A
Workstation	Windows 8 Enterprise	WKSTN-MBR-B
Workstation	Windows 8 Enterprise	WKSTN-MBR-C

In addition to the computers, you will also need the software listed in Table 5-2 to complete Lab 5.

Table 5-2
Software Required for Lab 5

Software	*Location*
Lab 5 student worksheet	Lab05_worksheet.docx (provided by instructor)

Working with Lab Worksheets

Each lab in this manual requires that you answer questions, create screenshots, and perform other activities that you will document in a worksheet named for the lab, such as Lab05_worksheet.docx. You will find these worksheets on the book companion site. It is recommended that you use a USB flash drive to store your worksheets so you can submit them to your instructor for review. As you perform the exercises in each lab, open the appropriate worksheet file using Word, type the required information, and then save the file to your flash drive.

SCENARIO

After completing this lab, you will be able to:

- Set Windows 8 file associations
- Set compatibility modes
- Modify file associations

Estimated lab time: 60 minutes

Exercise 5.1	Setting File Associations
Overview	In this exercise, you will demonstrate how you can use file associations to control which application loads when you execute a file of a particular type.
Mindset	Windows 8 uses file types to associate data files with specific applications. File can also appear as file name extensions.
Completion time	20 minutes

1. On **WKSTN-MBR-C**, log on using the **adatum\Student** account and the **Pa$$w0rd** password.

2. Click the **Desktop** tile. The *Desktop* appears.

3. In the taskbar, click the **File Explorer** icon. The *File Explorer* window appears.

4. Expand the **Computer** container and then select the **Local Disk (C:)** drive.

5. In the *Search Local Disk (C:)* box, type **jpg** and wait as the program searches the disk for JPG files.

6. Scroll down in the results list and double-click the **IMG104** file. The file opens in Photo.

7. Mouse over the lower-left corner of the window, right-click the **Start** screen thumbnail, and, from the context menu that appears, click **Control Panel**. The *Control Panel* window appears.

8. Click **Programs** > **Default Programs** > **Associate a file type or protocol with a program**. The *Associate a file type or protocol with a specific program* control panel appears (see Figure 5-1).

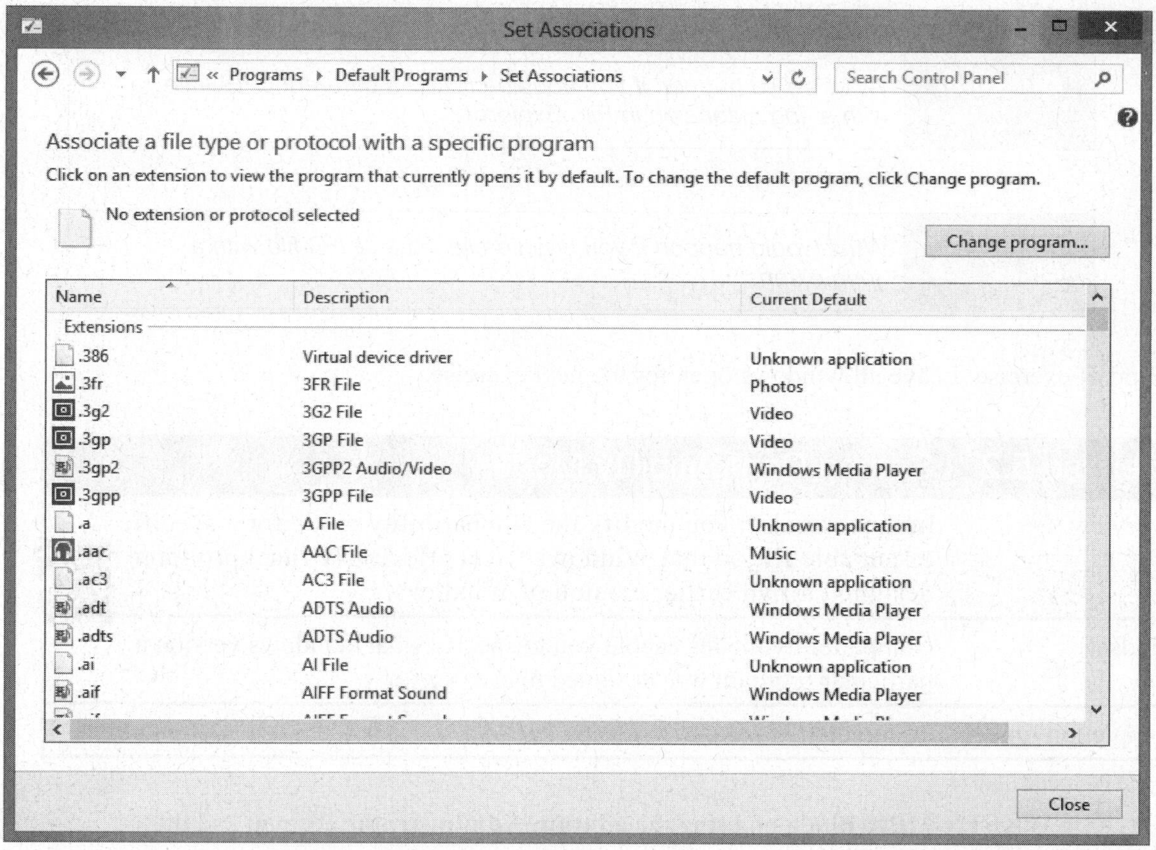

Figure 5-1
The Associate a file type or protocol with a specific program control panel

9. Scroll down in the list and select the **.jpg** file name extension.

Question 1	*What program is currently associated with the .jpg file name extension?*

10. Click **Change program**. The *How do you want to open this type of file (.jpg)?* dialog box appears.

11. Click **Windows Photo Viewer**. The default file association for the .jpg extension changes to *Windows Photo Viewer*.

12. Switch back to the *File Explorer* window and then double-click the **IMG104** file again. The image appears again, but now in the *Windows Photo Viewer* application.

13. Take a screen shot of the *Windows Photo Viewer* window by pressing **Alt+Prt Scr** and then paste it into your Lab 5 worksheet file in the page provided by pressing **Ctrl+V**.

Question 2	*What would happen if you double-clicked a different JPEG file with a .jpg extension in File Explorer?*

Question 3	*What would happen if you double-clicked a JPEG file with a .jpeg extension?*

End of exercise. Leave all windows open for the next exercise.

Exercise 5.2	Setting Compatibility Modes
Overview	In this exercise, you modify the compatibility mode for a specific executable file so that Windows 8 can effectively run a program designed for an earlier version of Windows.
Mindset	Compatibility modes enable you to specify what Windows version a particular program was designed to use.
Completion time	20 minutes

1. On **WKSTN-MBR-B**, log on using the **adatum\Administrator** account and the **Pa$$w0rd** password.

2. On the *Start* screen, click the **Desktop** tile. The *Desktop* appears.

3. On the taskbar, click the **File Explorer** button. The *File Explorer* window appears.

4. Expand the **Network** container and browse to the **\\SVR-DC-A\Downloads** folder.

5. Copy the **WinXP-SOL** folder to the **C:\Users\Administrator\Downloads** folder on **WKSTN-MBR-B**.

6. In the **C:\Users\Administrator\Downloads\WinXP-SOL** folder, right-click the **Sol** file and, from the context menu, choose **Properties**. The *sol Properties* sheet appears.

7. Click the *Compatibility* tab (see Figure 5-2).

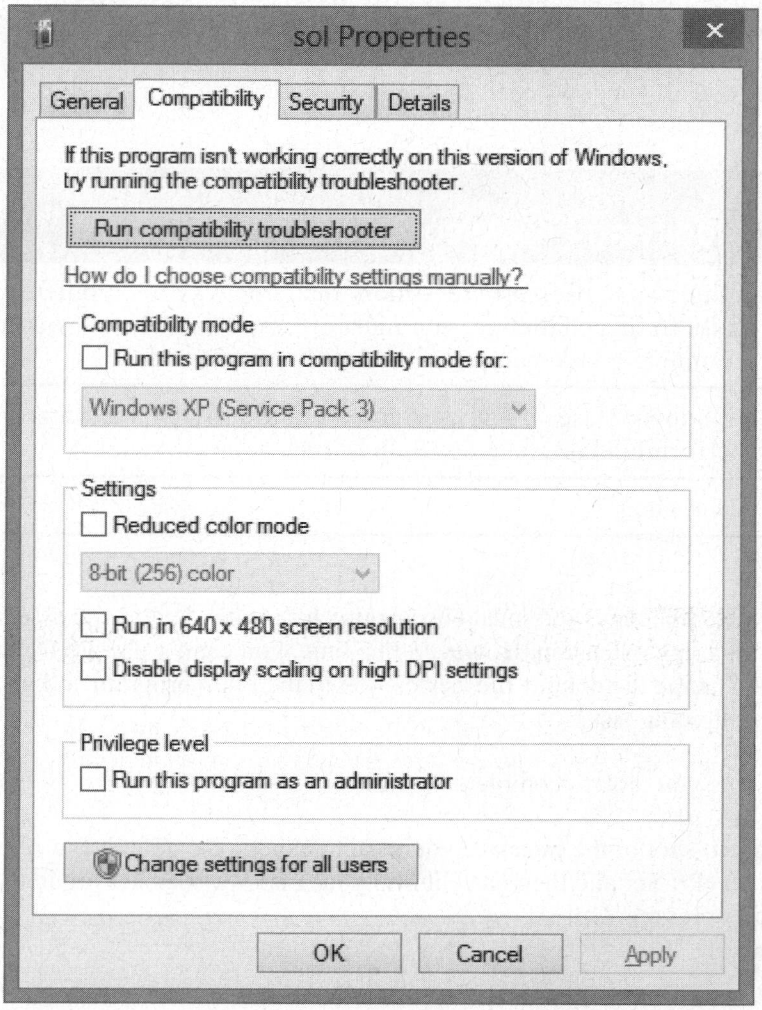

Figure 5-2
The Compatibility tab of the sol Properties sheet

8. Select the **Run this program in compatibility mode for** check box and, in the drop-down list, click **Windows XP (Service Pack 3)**.

Question 4	*What can you do if you are unsure which version of Windows you should specify in the compatibility settings?*

9. Click **OK**.

10. In *File Explorer*, double-click the **Sol** file. The *Solitaire* game screen appears.

11. Take a screen shot of the *Solitaire* window by pressing **Alt+Prt Scr** and then paste it into your Lab 5 worksheet file in the page provided by pressing **Ctrl+V**.

End of exercise. Leave all windows open for the next exercise.

Lab Challenge	Modifying File Associations
Overview	Windows 8 often provides more than one way to complete a given task. In this challenge, you must discover an alternate way to complete a task you performed earlier in this lab.
Mindset	Windows 8 uses its modern interface to provide alternative ways of performing tasks usually found in the Control Panel.
Completion time	20 minutes

To complete this challenge, you must once again change the default file association for JPEG files with a .jpg extension. However, this time, you cannot use the Default Programs control panel. Change the default file association to the Paint program and, in doing so, complete the following tasks:

1. List the steps you took to complete the task.

2. Take a screen shot of the interface you used to change the default file association by pressing Alt+Prt Scr and then paste it into your Lab 5 worksheet file in the page provided by pressing Ctrl+V.

End of lab.

LAB 6
INSTALLING AND CONFIGURING WINDOWS STORE APPLICATIONS

THIS LAB CONTAINS THE FOLLOWING EXERCISES AND ACTIVITIES:

Exercise 6.1	Using Group Policy to Restrict Access to the Windows Store
Exercise 6.2	Disabling Automatic Download Updates of the Windows Store
Lab Challenge	Blocking Automatic Updates from Within the Windows Store App

BEFORE YOU BEGIN

The lab environment consists of student workstations connected to a local area network, along with a server that functions as the domain controller for a domain called adatum.com. The computers required for this lab are listed in Table 6-1.

Table 6-1
Computers Required for Lab 6

Computer	*Operating System*	*Computer Name*
Server	Windows Server 2012	SVR-DC-A
Client	Windows 8 Enterprise	WKSTN-MBR-B
Client	Windows 7 Enterprise	WKSTN-MBR-C

In addition to the computers, you will also need the software listed in Table 6-2 to complete Lab 6.

Table 6-2
Software Required for Lab 6

Software	***Location***
Administrative Templates for Windows 8 and Windows Server 2012 (Windows8-Server2012ADMX-RTM.msi)	\\SVC-DC-A\Downloads
Lab 6 student worksheet	Lab06_worksheet.docx (provided by instructor)

Working with Lab Worksheets

Each lab in this manual requires that you answer questions, shoot screen shots, and perform other activities that you will document in a worksheet named for the lab, such as Lab06_worksheet.docx. You will find these worksheets on the book companion site. It is recommended that you use a USB flash drive to store your worksheets so you can submit them to your instructor for review. As you perform the exercises in each lab, open the appropriate worksheet file, type the required information, and then save the file to your flash drive.

SCENARIO

After completing this lab, you will be able to:

- Restrict access to the Windows Store
- Disable Automatic Download Updates of the Store
- Block automatic updates from within the Windows Store app

Estimated lab time: 35 minutes

Exercise 6.1	Using Group Policy to Restrict Access to the Windows Store
Overview	In this exercise, you will install the Windows 8/Windows Server 2012 Administrative Templates and then use GPOs to restrict access to the Windows Store.
Mindset	To maintain security within an organization, you may choose to restrict users from using the Store to download and install applications.
Completion time	20 minutes

1. On **SVR-DC-A**, log on using the **adatum\administrator** account and the **Pa$$w0rd** password.

2. Open **File Explorer** and navigate to the **\\SVR-DC-A\Downloads** folder.

3. Double-click the **Windows8-Server2012ADMX-RTM.msi** file. When you are prompted to confirm that you want to run this file, click **Run**.

4. When the *Administrative Templates for Windows Server 2012 Setup Wizard* opens, click **Next**.

5. On the *License Agreement* page, click **I Agree** and then click **Next**.

6. On the *Select Installation folder* page, click **Everyone**.

Question 1	*What is the default installation folder?*

7. Click **Next**.

8. On the *Confirm Installation* page, click **Next**.

9. When the installation is complete, click **Close**.

10. Using **File Explorer**, open the **C:\Program Files (x86)\Microsoft Group Policy\Windows Server2012** folder. Right-click the **PolicyDefinitions** folder and choose **Copy**.

11. Using **File Explorer**, open **\\SVR-DC-A\sysvol\adatum.com\Policies** (see Figure 6-1).

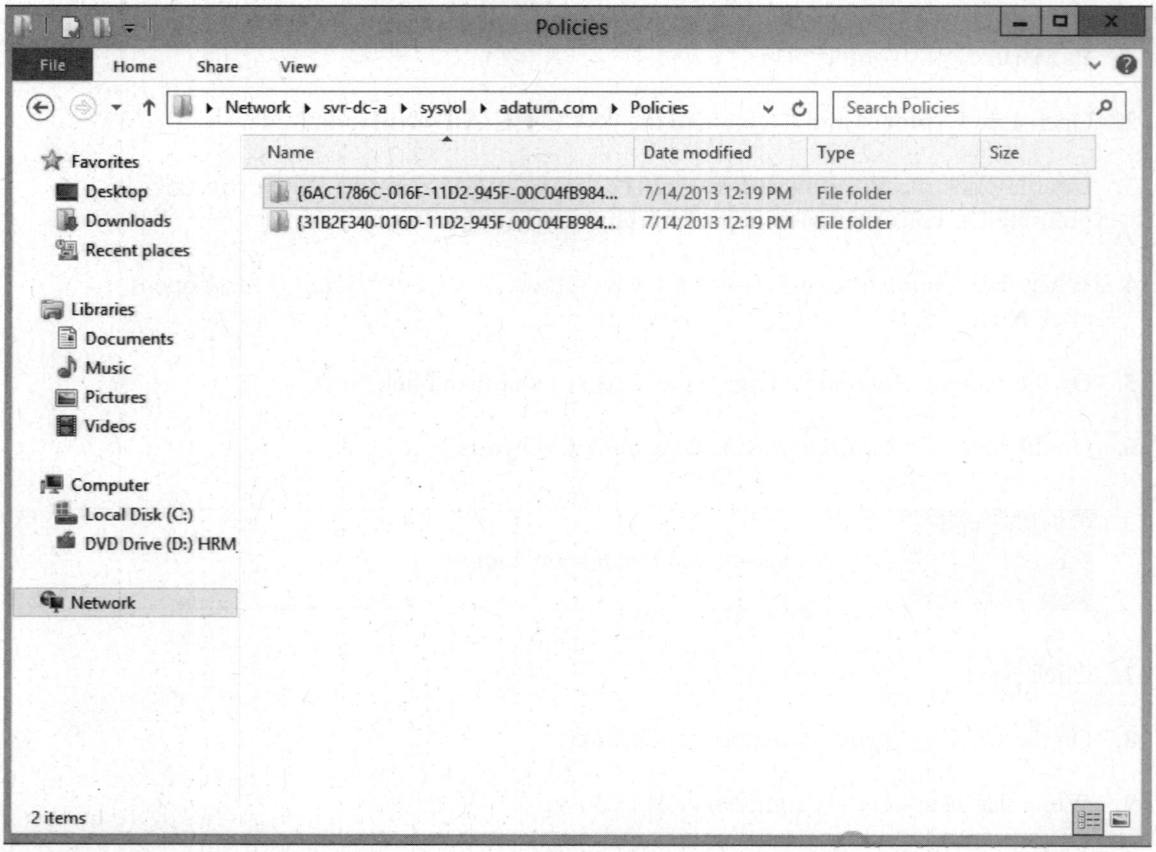

Figure 6-1
The Policies folder on a domain controller

12. In the *Policies* folder, right-click the empty white space and choose **Paste**.

13. Using **Server Manager**, click **Tools** > **Group Policy Management**.

14. When *Group Policy Management* opens, expand the **Forest: adatum.com** node, expand the **Domains** node, and then expand **adatum.com**.

15. Right-click the **Default Domain Policy** and choose **Edit**.

16. When the *Group Policy Management Editor* opens, navigate to **Computer Configuration > Policies > Administrative Templates > Windows Components > Store**.

17. Double-click the **Turn off the Store application setting**. The *Turn off the Store application* dialog displays. Click **Enabled**.

18. Press **Ctrl+Prt Scr** to take a screen shot that captures both the *Turn off the Store application* dialog box and the *Group Policy Management Editor* window. Press **Ctrl+V** to paste the image on the page provided in the Lab 6 worksheet file.

19. Click **OK** to close the *Turn off the Store application* dialog box. The next time the group policy settings are replicated to the client, the store will be disabled.

End of exercise. Leave the Group Policy Management Editor open for the next exercise.

Exercise 6.2	Disabling Automatic Download Updates of the Windows Store
Overview	In this exercise, you will use a GPO to disable the automatic downloading of updates from the Windows store.
Mindset	Sometimes, updates can cause unforeseen problems. To avoid some of these problems, you can stop applications from downloading and installing updates for Windows Store applications.
Completion time	10 minutes

1. On **SVR-DC-A**, using **Group Policy Management Editor**, navigate to **Computer Configuration > Policies > Administrative Templates > Windows Components > Store** (see Figure 6-2).

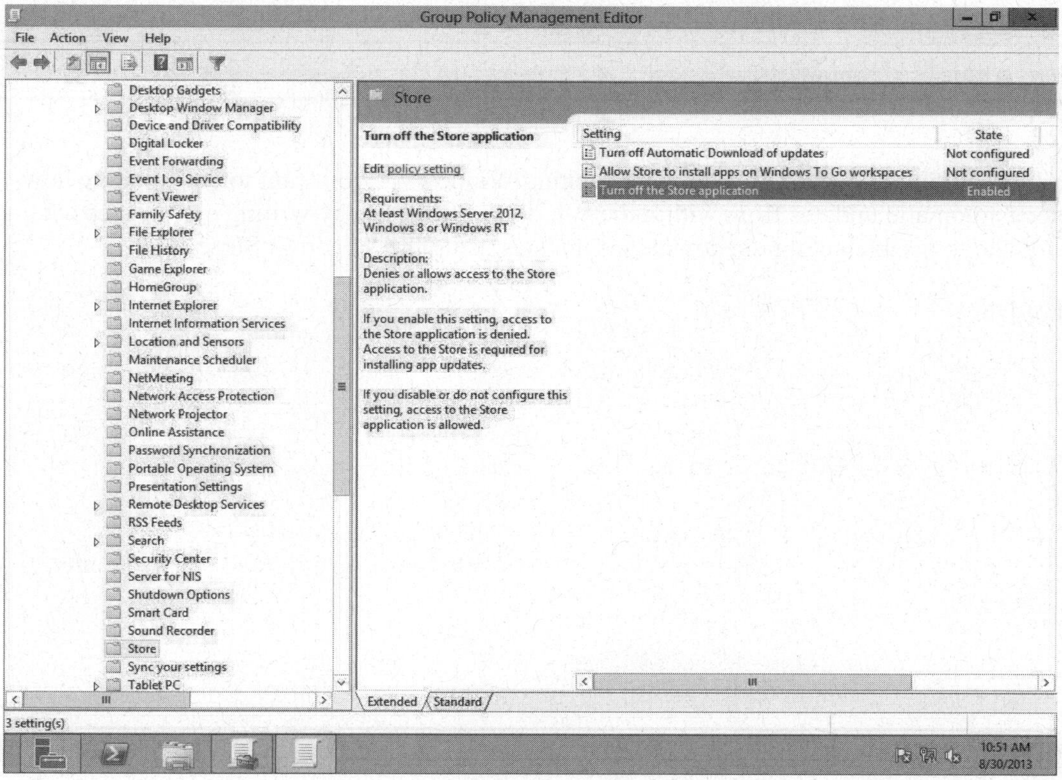

Figure 6-2
A GPO showing the *Store* node

2. Double-click **Turn off Automatic Download of updates**.

3. For the policy setting, select **Enabled**.

4. Press **Ctrl+Prt Scr** to take a screen shot of the *Turn off Automatic Download of updates* dialog box and the *Group Policy Management Editor* window. Press **Ctrl+V** to paste the image on the page provided in the Lab 6 worksheet file.

5. Click **OK** to close the *Turn off Automatic Download of updates* dialog box.

6. Close **Group Policy Management Editor** and then close **Group Policy Management**.

End of exercise.

Lab Challenge	Blocking Automatic Updates from within the Windows Store App
Overview	In this lab challenge, you will demonstrate how to disable automatic download updates using the Windows Store App.
Mindset	You have a local computer that is sensitive and you do not want to deploy any updates or changes to the system unless you manually update or change the system.
Completion time	5 minutes

As a local administrator for the computer running Windows 8, you want to demonstrate how to block automatic updates from within the Windows Store App by writing out the steps that it would take to disable automatic downloads updates using the Windows Store app.

End of lab.

LAB 7
CONTROLLING ACCESS TO LOCAL HARDWARE AND APPLICATIONS

THIS LAB CONTAINS THE FOLLOWING EXERCISES AND ACTIVITIES:

Exercise 7.1	Installing Remote Server Administration Tools
Exercise 7.2	Configuring Removable Storage Access Policies
Exercise 7.3	Using AppLocker
Lab Challenge	Creating an AppLocker Rule Based on File Hash

BEFORE YOU BEGIN

The lab environment consists of student workstations connected to a local area network, along with a server that functions as the domain controller for a domain called adatum.com. The computers required for this lab are listed in Table 7-1.

Table 7-1
Computers Required for Lab 7

Computer	*Operating System*	*Computer Name*
Server	Windows Server 2012	SVR-DC-A
Client	Windows 8 Enterprise	WKSTN-MBR-B

In addition to the computers, you will also need the software listed in Table 7-2 to complete Lab 7.

Table 7-2
Software Required for Lab 7

Software	*Location*
Remote Server Administration Tools for Windows 8 (Windows6.2-KB2693643-x64.msu)	\\SVR-DC-A\Downloads
Lab 7 student worksheet	Lab07_worksheet.docx (provided by instructor)

Working with Lab Worksheets

Each lab in this manual requires that you answer questions, shoot screen shots, and perform other activities that you will document in a worksheet named for the lab, such as Lab07_worksheet.docx. You will find these worksheets on the book companion site. It is recommended that you use a USB flash drive to store your worksheets so you can submit them to your instructor for review. As you perform the exercises in each lab, open the appropriate worksheet file, type the required information, and then save the file to your flash drive.

SCENARIO

After completing this lab, you will be able to:

- Install the Remote Server Administration Tools on a computer running Windows 8
- Configure a Removable Storage Access Policy
- Use AppLocker to restrict software applications for a user

Estimated lab time: 60 minutes

Exercise 7.1	Installing Remote Server Administration Tools
Overview	In this exercise, you will install the Remote Server Administration Tools on a computer running Windows 8 so that you can use Active Directory tools and other administrative tools on a Windows 8 workstation.
Mindset	Since users work from their client computers, it is always convenient to have the Remote Server Administration Tools available on the administrator's client computer.
Completion time	20 minutes

1. On **WKSTN-MBR-B**, log on using the **adatum\Administrator** account and the **Pa$$w0rd** password.

2. Click the **Desktop** tile.

3. On the Taskbar, click the **File Explorer** icon.

4. When *File Explorer* opens, open the **\\SVR-DC-A\downloads** folder (see Figure 7-1).

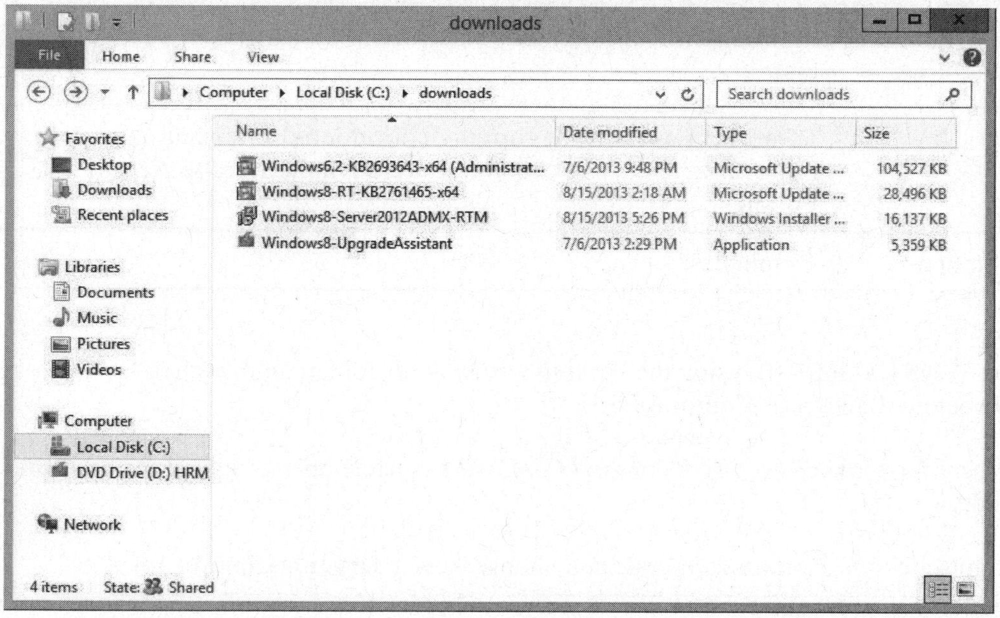

Figure 7-1
The *Downloads* folder

5. Double-click the **Windows6.2-KB2693643-x64.msu** file.

6. If you are prompted to install this file, click **Open**. When you are prompted to install the Windows software update, click **Yes**.

7. On the *Read these license terms* page, click **I Accept**.

8. If you are prompted to restart the computer, click **Restart Now**.

9. If you need to restart, then after rebooting, log back in to **WKSTN-MBR-B** as **adatum\Administrator** using the **Pa$$w0rd** password.

10. Scroll to the right and then click the **Administrative Tools** tile.

Question 1	*Which two tools are used to administer users for Active Directory?*

11. Take a screen shot of the *Administrative Tools* window by pressing **Alt+Prt Scr** and then paste the resulting image into the Lab 7 worksheet file in the page provided by pressing **Ctrl+V**.

End of exercise. Leave the system logged in for the next exercise.

Exercise 7.2	Configuring Removable Storage Access Policies
Overview	In this exercise, you will restrict the ability to write to an optical disk.
Mindset	To prevent users from copying confidential information to a removable disk, you can create Removable Storage Access Policies.
Completion time	15 minutes

1. On **WKSTN-MBR-B**, using the *Administrative Tools* folder, double-click **Active Directory Users and Computers**.

2. When the *Active Directory Users and Computers* console opens, expand the **adatum.com** node.

3. Right-click the **adatum.com** node and choose **New > Organizational Unit**.

4. When the *New Object – Organizational Unit* dialog box displays, in the *Name* text box, type **Restricted**.

5. Click **OK** to close the *New Object – Organizational Unit* dialog box.

6. Close **Active Directory Users and Computers**.

7. Go back to the *Administrative Tools* folder and double-click **Group Policy Management**.

8. When the *Group Policy Management* console opens, expand the **Forest: adatum.com** node, expand the **Domains** node, expand the **adatum.com** node, and then expand the **Group Policy Objects** node (see Figure 7-2).

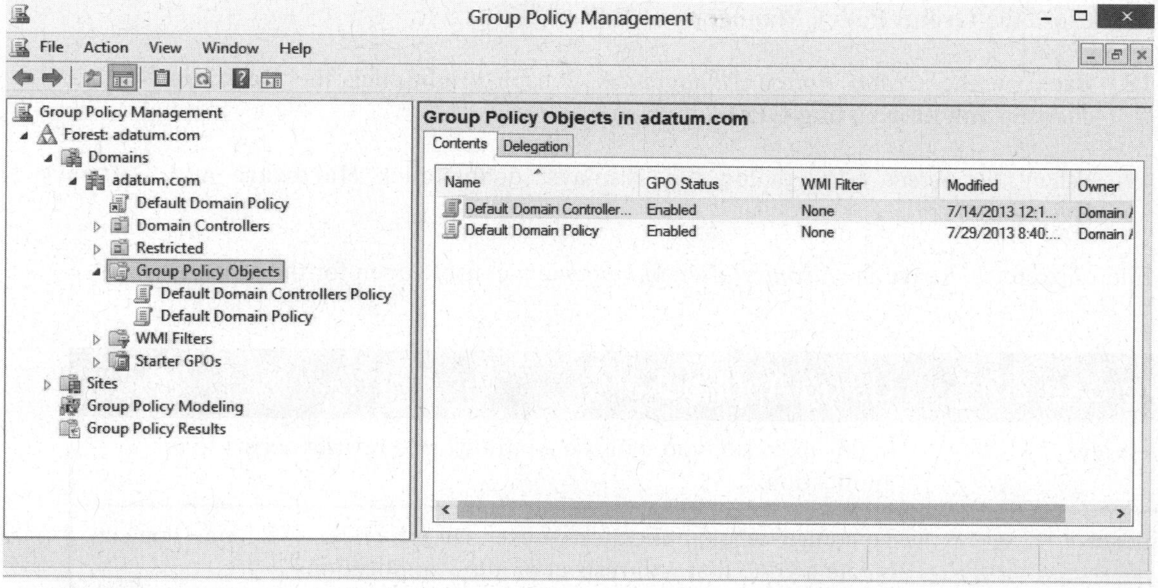

Figure 7-2
The *Group Policy Objects* node

9. Right-click **Group Policy Objects** and choose **New**.

10. When the *New GPO* window displays, in the *Name* text box, type **Hardware and Software Restrictions**, and then click **OK**.

11. Right-click the **Hardware and Software Restrictions** GPO and choose **Edit**.

12. When the *Group Policy Management Editor* window opens, under the **User Configuration** node, expand the **Policies** node, expand the **Administrative Templates**, expand the **System** node, and then click the **Removable Storage Access** node.

Question 2	*Which policy setting prevents writing to a USB device?*

13. To stop writing to writable optical disk, in the right pane, double-click **CD and DVD: Deny Write access**.

14. When the *CD and DVD: Deny write access* dialog box displays, click the **Enabled** option.

15. Click **OK** to close the *CD and DVD: Deny write access* dialog box.

16. Take a screen shot of the *Group Policy Management Editor* window by pressing **Alt+Prt Scr** and then paste the resulting image into the Lab 7 worksheet file in the page provided by pressing **Ctrl+V**.

17. Close the **Group Policy Management Editor**.

18. Back on the *Group Policy Management* console, right-click the **Restricted** OU and choose **Link an Existing GPO**.

19. When the *Select GPO* dialog box displays, double-click **Hardware and Software Restrictions**.

End of exercise. Leave the *Group Policy Management* console open for the next exercise.

Exercise 7.3	Using AppLocker
Overview	In this exercise, you will use AppLocker to restrict access to an application.
Mindset	To control what applications a user can run on her machine, you can create a GPO that will restrict or allow applications.
Completion time	15 minutes

1. On **WKSTN-MBR-B**, using the *Group Policy Management* console, under the Group Policy Objects node, right-click the **Hardware and Software Restricted** GPO and then choose click **Edit**.

2. When the *Group Policy Management Editor* console displays, browse to the **Computer Configuration\Policies\Windows Settings\Security Settings\Application Control Policies** container and then click the **AppLocker** node.

3. Expand the **AppLocker** container and then click the **Executable Rules** node (see Figure 7-3).

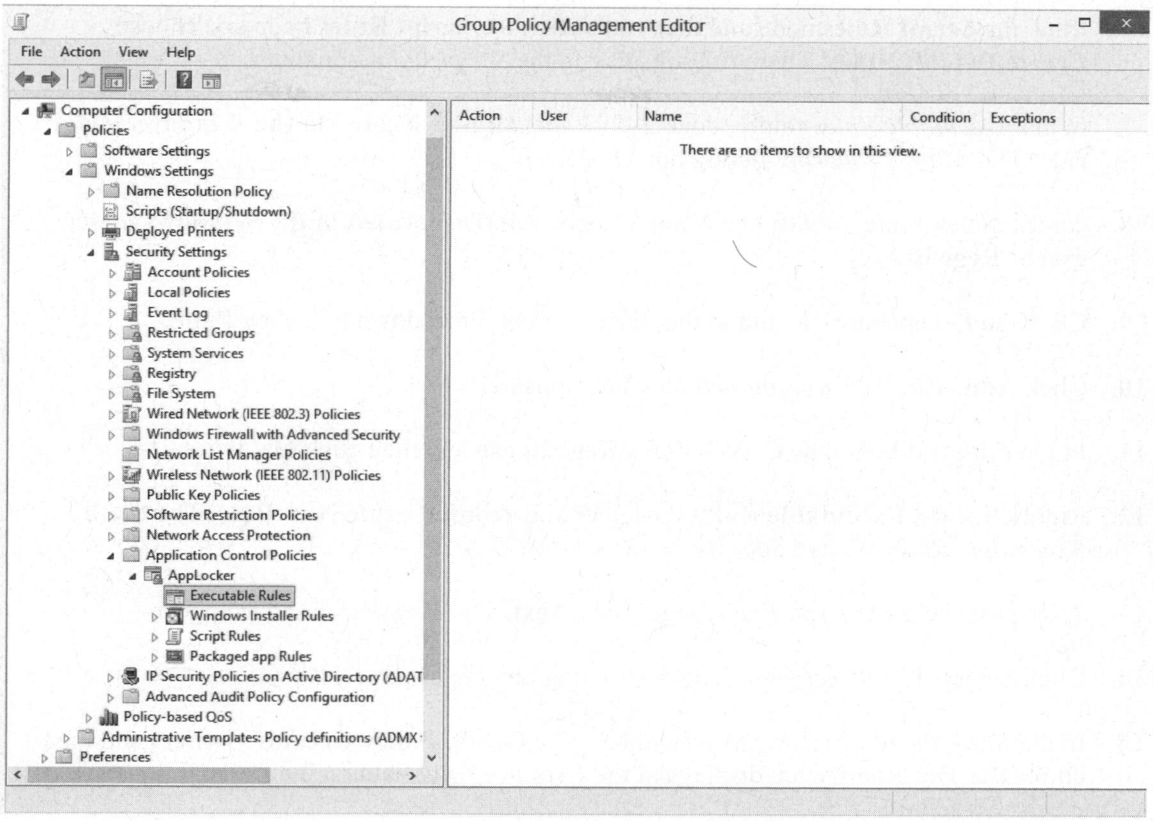

Figure 7-3
A GPO that shows the AppLocker Executable Rules node

4. Right-click the **Executable Rules** node and choose **Create Default Rules**. Three rules display in the *Executable Rules* container.

Question 3	*Based on the default rules that appear in the Executable Rules folder, which programs can a typical user run on a Windows 8 workstation? Which programs can members of the Administrators group run?*

5. Click the **Windows Installer Rules** node and then right-click the **Windows Installer Rules** node and choose **Create Default Rules**. Three rules display in the *Windows Installer Rules* container.

Question 4	*Based on the default rules that appear in the Windows Installer Rules folder, which Windows Installer files can a typical user run on a Windows 8 workstation? Which Windows Installer files can members of the Administrators group run?*

6. Click the **Script Rules** node and then right-click the **Script Rules** node and choose **Create Default Rules**. Three rules display in the *Script Rules* container.

7. In the *Executable Rules* folder, double-click the **All files located in the Windows folder rule**. The *Allow Properties* dialog box appears.

8. On the *General* tab, modify the *Name* value to **All files located in the Windows folder except Regedit.exe**.

9. Click the **Exceptions** tab, and in the *Add exception* drop-down list, click **Path**.

10. Click **Add**. The *Path Exception* dialog box appears.

11. In the *Path* text box, type **C:\Windows\Regedit.exe** and then click **OK** twice.

12. Right-click the **Executable Rules** container and choose **Create New Rule**. The *Create Executable Rules* Wizard appears.

13. To bypass the *Before You Begin* page, click **Next**. The *Permissions* page appears.

14. Click **Select**. The *Select User or Group* dialog box appears.

15. In the *Enter the object name to select* box, type **Group Policy Creator Owners** and then click **OK**. The group name displays in the *User or group* field on the *Permissions* page.

16. Click **Next**. The *Conditions* page appears.

17. Select the **Path** option and then click **Next**. The *Path* page appears.

18. In the *Path* text box, type **C:\Windows\Regedit.exe** and then click **Create**. The new rule displays in the *Executable Rules* container.

Question 5	*Why is it necessary to create the additional rule for the Group Policy Creator Owners group?*

19. Take a screen shot of the *Group Policy Management Editor* console displaying the contents of the *Executable Rules* container by pressing **Alt+Prt Scr** and then paste the resulting image into the Lab 7 worksheet file in the page provided by pressing **Ctrl+V**.

End of exercise. Leave the Group Policy Management console and Group Policy Editor for the Hardware and Software Restricted GPO open for the next exercise.

Lab Challenge	Creating an AppLocker Rule Based on File Hash
Overview	In this exercise, you will create a rule that will deny users from running the Math Input Panel (mip.exe) based on the file hash.
Mindset	Sometimes, when administrators block a file based on a specific path, some users will try to install or copy a file to a different folder and run the program from there. You can block a file based on file hash, which will stop the program from running no matter where it is being executed from.
Completion time	10 minutes

During this exercise, you will create an AppLocker rule that will deny users from running the Math Input Panel based on file hash. The Math Input Panel file is located at C:\Program Files\Common\microsoft shared\ink\mip.exe. Write out the procedure you used to configure the settings, and then take a screen shot of the container where the settings are located by pressing **Alt+Prt Scr** and then paste the resulting image into the Lab 7 worksheet file in the page provided by pressing **Ctrl+V**.

End of lab.

LAB 8 CONFIGURING INTERNET EXPLORER

THIS LAB CONTAINS THE FOLLOWING EXERCISES AND ACTIVITIES:

Exercise 8.1	Configuring Internet Explorer
Exercise 8.2	Testing Internet Explorer Policies
Lab Challenge	Suppressing Compatibility Warnings

BEFORE YOU BEGIN

The lab environment consists of student workstations connected to a local area network, along with a server that functions as the domain controller for a domain called adatum.com. The computers required for this lab are listed in Table 8-1.

Table 8-1
Computers Required for Lab 8

Computer	*Operating System*	*Computer Name*
Server	Windows Server 2012	SVR-DC-A
Client	Windows 8 Enterprise	WKSTN-MBR-B

In addition to the computers, you will also need the software listed in Table 8-2 to complete Lab 8.

Table 8-2
Software Required for Lab 8

Software	*Location*
Lab 8 student worksheet	Lab08_worksheet.docx (provided by instructor)

Working with Lab Worksheets

Each lab in this manual requires that you answer questions, shoot screen shots, and perform other activities that you will document in a worksheet named for the lab, such as Lab08_worksheet.docx. You will find these worksheets on the book companion site. It is recommended that you use a USB flash drive to store your worksheets so you can submit them to your instructor for review. As you perform the exercises in each lab, open the appropriate worksheet file, type the required information, and then save the file to your flash drive.

SCENARIO

After completing this lab, you will be able to:

- Configure Internet Explorer settings using Group Policy.
- Test Internet Explorer policies
- Suppress compatibility warnings

Estimated lab time: 50 minutes

Exercise 8.1	Configuring Internet Explorer
Overview	In this exercise, you will configure Internet Explorer using Group Policy.
Mindset	As an administrator, you need to ensure that Internet Explorer is configured based on the policy of your organization. To configure IE for the entire organization, you can use Group Policy.
Completion time	20 minutes

1. On **WKSTN-MBR-B**, log on using the **adatum\administrator** account and the **Pa$$w0rd** password.

2. On the **Start** screen, scroll to the right, click **Administrative Tools,** and then double-click **Group Policy Management**.

3. When the *Group Policy Management* console displays, expand **Forest:adatum.com**, expand **Domains**, expand **adatum.com**, expand the **Restricted** OU, and then click the **Hardware and Software Restriction** GPO.

4. Right-click the **Hardware and Software Restrictions** GPO and choose **Edit**. The *Group Policy Management Editor* console appears.

5. Browse to the **User Configuration\Policies\Administrative Templates\Windows Components\Internet Explorer** container (see figure 8-1).

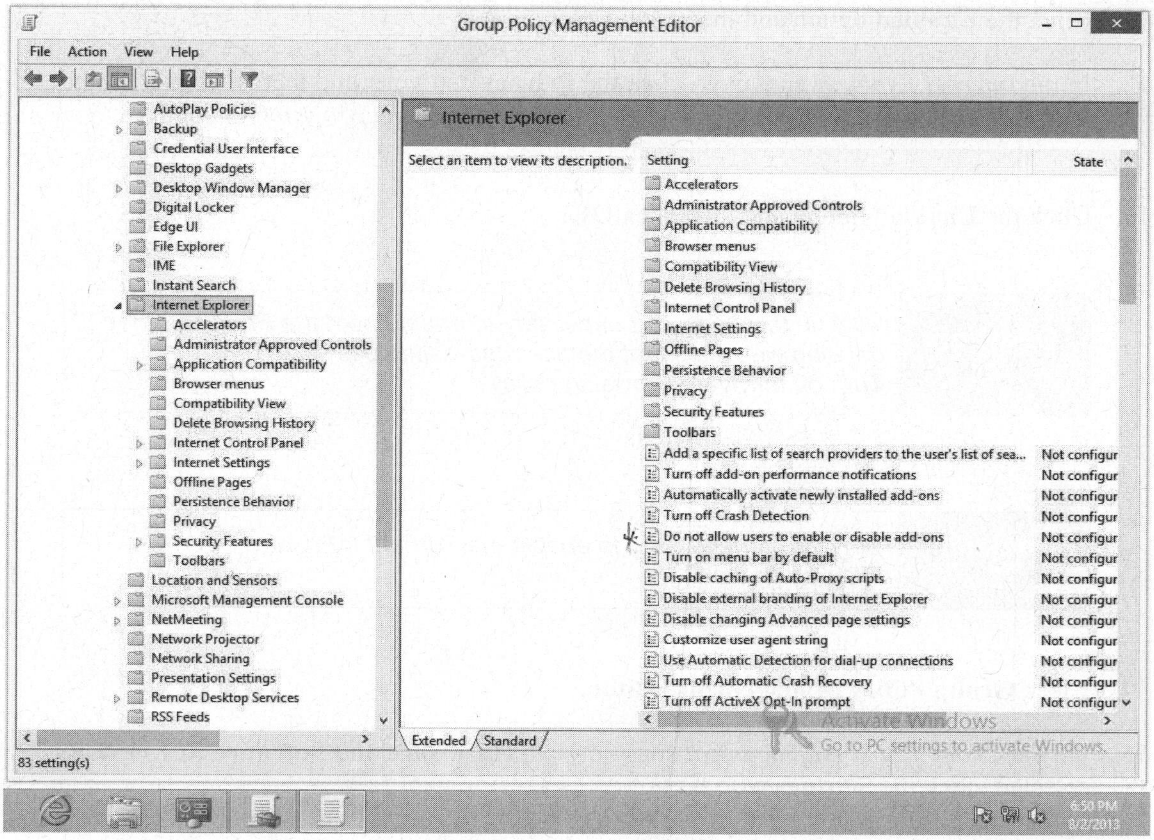

Figure 8-1
The Internet Explorer GPO settings

6. Double-click the **Do not allow users to enable or disable add-ons** policy. The *Do not allow users to enable or disable add-ons* dialog box appears.

7. Click **Enabled** and then click **OK**.

8. In the *Internet Explorer* container, select the **Compatibility View** container and then double-click the **Turn on Internet Explorer 7 Standards Mode for local intranet** policy. The *Turn on Internet Explorer 7 Standards Mode for local intranet* dialog box appears.

9. Select **Disabled** and then click **OK**.

Question 1	*Why is it necessary to disable the Turn on Internet Explorer Standards Mode for Local Intranet policy?*

10. In the *Internet Explorer* container, click the **Delete Browsing History** container and then double-click the **Prevent deleting web sites that the user has visited** policy. The *Prevent deleting web sites that the user has visited* dialog box appears.

11. Click the **Enabled** option and then click **OK**.

12. In the *Internet Explorer* container, click the **Privacy** container and then double-click the **Turn off InPrivate Browsing** policy. The *Turn off InPrivate Browsing* dialog box appears.

13. Click the **Enabled** option and then click **OK**.

Question 2	*Why, in this case, is it necessary to enable both the Prevent deleting web sites that the user has visited policy and the Turn off InPrivate Browsing policy?*

Question 3	*Why isn't it necessary to enable the Turn off InPrivate Filtering as well?*

14. Close **Group Policy Management Editor**.

15. On the *Group Policy Management* console, with **Hardware and Software Restrictions** selected, click the **Settings** tab.

16. Under *User Configuration*, click **Administrative Templates**.

17. Take a screen shot of the *Group Policy Management* console displaying all of the policy settings you configured in this exercise by pressing **Alt+Prt Scr** and then paste the resulting image into the Lab 8 worksheet file in the page provided by pressing **Ctrl+V**.

18. Close the **Group Policy Management** console.

End of exercise. Leave the console open and the computer logged on for the next exercise.

Exercise 8.2	Testing Internet Explorer Policies
Overview	In this exercise, you will confirm the Internet Explorer settings that are configured with a GPO are deployed to a client computer.
Mindset	When troubleshooting problems, you will need to ensure that settings that you configure with a GPO are actually deployed to the clients.
Completion time	20 minutes

1. On **WKSTN-MBR-B**, Using the **Administrative Tools** folder, double-click **Active Directory Users and Computers**.

2. Right-click the **Restricted** OU and choose **New > User**.

3. When the *New Object – User* dialog box displays, type the following information and then click **Next**:

   First name: **User**

   Last name: **1** User1 @adatum.com

   User logon name: **User1**

4. In the *Password* box and in the *Confirm Password* box, type **Pa$$w0rd**. Deselect **User must change password at next logon** and then select **Password never expires**. Click **Next**.

5. When the wizard is complete, click **Finish**.

6. Close **Active Directory Users and Computers**.

7. Log off as **adatum\administrator**.

8. Log on as **adatum\user1** with the **Pa$$w0rd** password.

9. Click the **Desktop** tile.

10. Log off as **adatum\user1**.

11. Logon as **adatum\administrator** with the **Pa$$w0rd** password.

12. Open the **Administrative Tools** folder and double-click **Group Policy Management**.

13. Click the **Group Policy Results** node (see Figure 8-2).

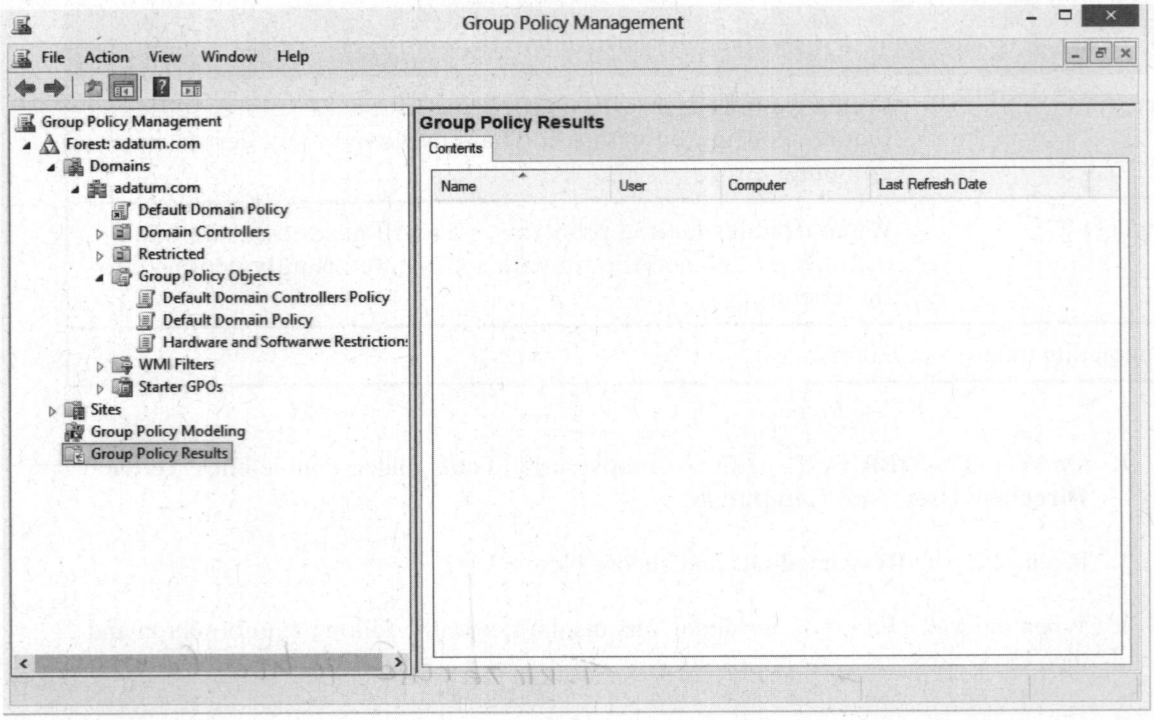

Figure 8-2
Opening the Group Policy Results node

14. Right-click the **Group Policy Results** node and choose **Group Policy Results Wizard**.

15. When the *Group Policy Results Wizard* starts, click **Next**.

16. On the *Computer Selection* page, click **Next**.

17. On the *User Selection* page, click to select the **Select a specific user** and then click **Adatum\User1**. Click **Next**.

18. On the *Summary of Selections* page, click **Next**.

19. When the wizard is complete, click **Finish**.

20. With **user1** on **WKSTN-MBR-B** selected, in the right pane, click the **Details** tab.

21. Examine the options to verify that User 1 is receiving the IE settings that you just set by clicking **show** next to **User Details, Settings, and Policies**.

22. Expand **show** next to **Windows Components/Internet Explorer** and **Windows Components/Internet Explorer/Compatibility View**.

23. Take a screen shot of the *Group Policy Management* console showing the Internet Explorer policy settings displayed with the Group Policy Results by pressing **Alt+Prt Scr** and then paste the resulting image into the Lab 8 worksheet file in the page provided by pressing **Ctrl+V**.

Question 4	*If you have confirmed GPO settings are configured correctly, and the GPO is assigned to the correct container, which command can be used to ensure that the GPO settings is deployed to the user immediately?*

24. Close **Group Policy Management Editor**.

End of exercise. Leave the Group Policy Management console open for the lab Challenge.

Lab Challenge	Suppressing Compatibility Warnings
Overview	To complete this challenge, you must demonstrate how to suppress the compatibility warnings.
Mindset	The Windows 8 users at Contoso, Ltd. are restricted to a predefined set of applications, all of which have been recently updated and carefully tested for compatibility. To prevent users from attempting to run down-level applications, you have been instructed to disable the Windows 7 compatibility mode controls using Group Policy.
Completion time	10 minutes

To complete this challenge, you must locate and configure the appropriate Group Policy settings to accomplish these goals in the GPO you created in Exercise 8.1. Write out the procedure you used to configure the settings, and then take a screen shot of the container where the settings are located by pressing **Alt+Prt Scr** and then paste the resulting image into the Lab 8 worksheet file in the page provided by pressing **Ctrl+V**.

End of lab.

LAB 9
CONFIGURING HYPER-V

THIS LAB CONTAINS THE FOLLOWING EXERCISES AND ACTIVITIES:

Exercise 9.1	Installing Client Hyper-V
Exercise 9.2	Creating a Virtual Machine Using Hyper-V Manager
Exercise 9.3	Configuring Virtual Machine Settings
Lab Challenge	Expanding a Virtual Hard Disk

BEFORE YOU BEGIN

The lab environment consists of computers connected to a local area network. The computers required for this lab are listed in Table 9-1.

Table 9-1
Computers Required for Lab 9

Computer	***Operating System***	***Computer Name***
Server	Windows Server 2012	SVR-DC-A
Client	Windows 8 Enterprise	WKSTN-MBR-B

In addition to the computers, you will also require the software listed in Table 9-2 to complete Lab 9.

Table 9-2
Software Required for Lab 9

Software	***Location***
Windows 8 installation ISO	\\SVR-DC-A\Software\.
Lab 9 student worksheet	Lab09_worksheet.docx (provided by instructor)

Working with Lab Worksheets

Each lab in this manual requires that you answer questions, create screen shots, and then perform other activities that you will document in a worksheet named for the lab, such as Lab09_worksheet.docx. You will find these worksheets on the book companion site. It is recommended that you use a USB flash drive to store your worksheets so you can submit them to your instructor for review. As you perform the exercises in each lab, open the appropriate worksheet file, type the required information, and then save the file to your flash drive.

SCENARIO

After completing this lab, you will be able to:

- Install and configure Hyper-V
- Create a virtual machine in Hyper-V
- Take a snapshot of a virtual machine and then delete a snapshot of a virtual machine

Estimated lab time: 45 minutes

Exercise 9.1	Installing Client Hyper-V
Overview	In this exercise, you will install Hyper-V on a computer running Windows 8.
Mindset	Sometimes an older application will not work on Windows 8, even though you use the Compatibility Troubleshooter. One solution is to install Hyper-V on the client computer, create a virtual machine, and then install Windows XP on the virtual machine. You can then install and run the application on the virtual machine.
Completion time	15 minutes

1. On **WKSTN-MBR-B**, log on using the **adatum\administrator** account and the **Pa$$w0rd** password. Click the **Desktop** tile.
2. Mouse over the lower-left corner of the desktop and right-click the Start screen thumbnail that appears there. Then click **Command Prompt (Admin)**.
3. Since Windows 8 is running as a virtual machine, you will need to install Hyper-V using the DISM command. Therefore, execute the following command:

```
dism /online /enable-feature /featurename:Microsoft-Hyper-
V-All
```

4. When prompted to reboot the computer, type **Y**.

5. Log into WKSTN-MBR-B as **adatum\administrator** using the **Pa$$w0rd** password.

6. Click the **Desktop** tile.

7. Mouse over the lower-left corner of the desktop and right-click the Start screen thumbnail that appears there. Then click **Control Panel**.

8. Click **Programs**, and then in the *Programs* window, click **Turn Windows Features on or off**.

9. In the *Windows Features* window, expand **Hyper-V** and then expand **Hyper-V Management Tools**.

10. Take a screen shot of the *Windows Features* window by pressing **Alt+Prt Scr** and then paste it into your Lab 9 worksheet file in the page provided by pressing **Ctrl+V**.

11. Click **OK** to close the *Windows Features* window.

12. Close the *Programs and Features* window.

13. Mouse over the lower-left corner of the desktop and click the Start screen thumbnail that appears there. When the *Start* screen displays, scroll to the right and then click **Hyper-V Manager**.

14. When *Hyper-V Manager* opens, right-click **WKSTN-MBR-B** and then click **Virtual Switch Manager**.

15. When the *Virtual Switch Manager* appears (see Figure 9-1) in the right pane, where it prompts you do identify the type of virtual switch that you want to create, click **Internal**.

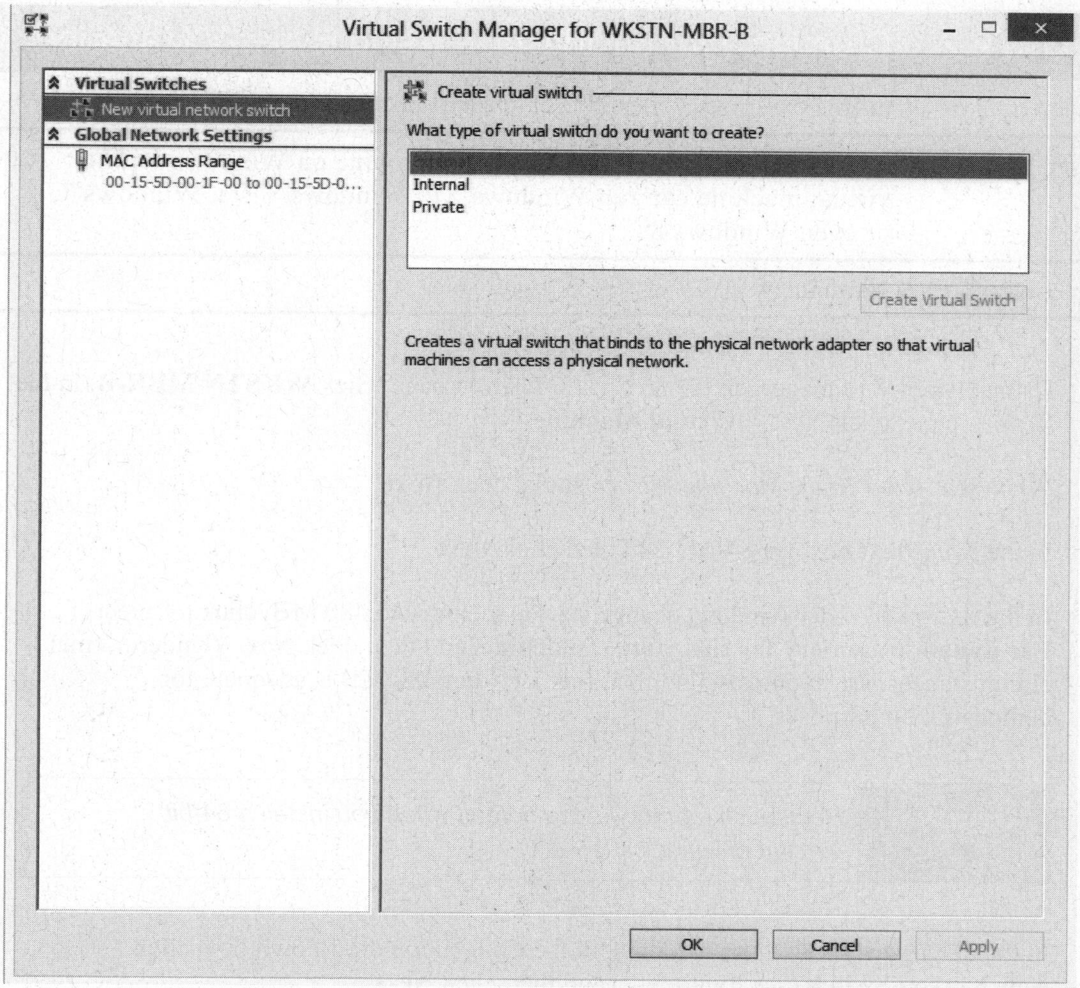

Figure 9-1
The Virtual Switch Manager

Question 1	*Which type of virtual switch would you select if you want the VM to connect to the Internet?*

16. Click **Create Virtual Switch**.

17. Click **OK** to close the *Virtual Switch Manager*.

End of exercise. Leave the computer on for the next exercise.

Exercise 9.2	Creating a Virtual Machine Using Hyper-V Manager
Overview	In this exercise, you will create a virtual machine in Hyper-V.
Mindset	Hyper-V allows you to run a virtual machine on Windows 8. The virtual machine can run Windows XP, Windows Vista, Windows 7, or even Windows 8.
Completion time	10 minutes

1. Using Hyper-V Manager, on the *Hyper-V Manager* page, click **WKSTN-MBR-B**. In the *Actions* pane, click **New** > **Virtual Machine**.

2. When the *New Virtual Machine Wizard* starts, click **Next**.

3. In the *Name* text box, type **VM1** and then click **Next**.

4. In the *Assign Memory* window, change startup memory to 480 MB, click to select **Use dynamic memory for this virtual machine**, and then click **Next**. (Under normal circumstances, you would assign more memory, but 480 MB is adequate for demonstration purposes.)

Question 2	*How much memory is the default when you install a 64-bit version of windows 8?*

5. In the *Configure Networking* window, in the *Connection* drop-down box, click **New Virtual Switch** (see Figure 9-2) and then click **Next**.

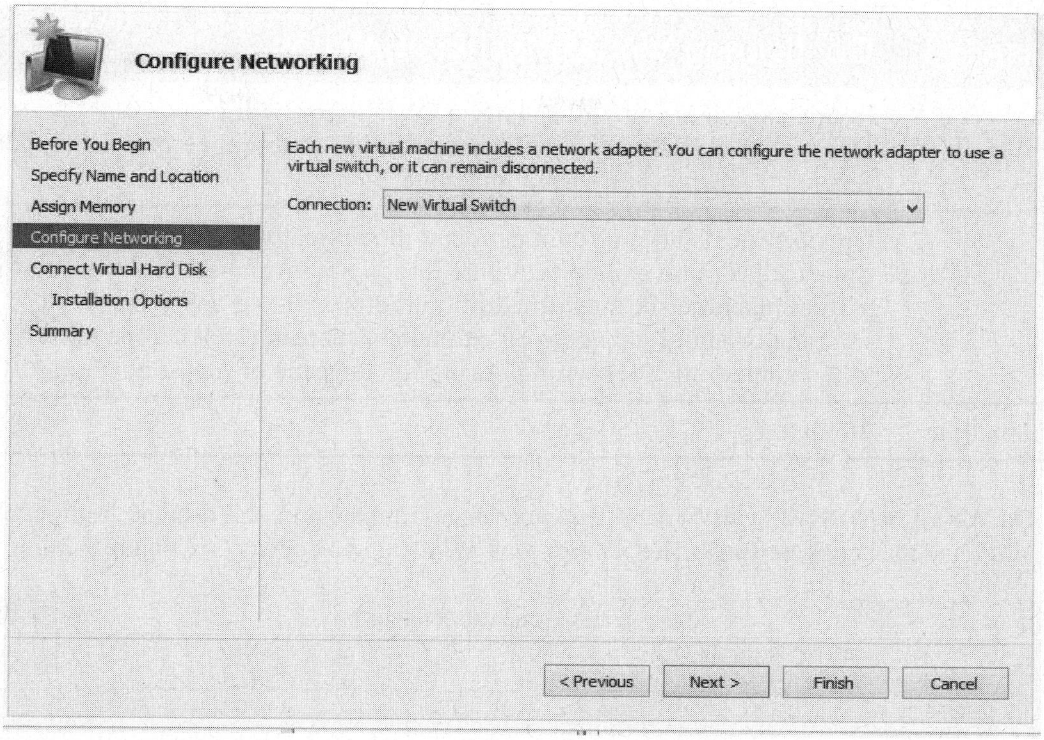

Figure 9-2
The *Configure Networking* page

6. In the *Connect Virtual Hard Disk* window, click to select **Create a virtual hard disk**, and then specify **5** GB for the size. Click **Next**. (Again, you would not normally use a small hard drive, but this setting is adequate for demonstration purposes.)

7. On the *Installation Options* page, click to select **Install an operating system later** and then click **Next**.

8. In the *Completing the New Virtual Machine Wizard* window, click **Finish**. Once completed, the new virtual machine appears in the Virtual Machines list of the Hyper-V Manager.

9. Take a screen shot of the *Hyper-V Manager* console showing the newly created VM by pressing **Alt+Prt Scr** and then paste it into your Lab 9 worksheet file in the page provided by pressing **Ctrl+V**.

Note	*Since we are running Hyper-V on a virtual machine, we will not be able to run virtual machines.*

End of exercise. Leave Hyper-V Manager open for the next exercise.

Exercise 9.3	Configuring Virtual Machine Settings
Overview	In this exercise, you will specify a DVD to use within a virtual machine. You will also create a snapshot of a virtual machine and then delete a snapshot of a virtual machine.
Mindset	On a physical server, you must open the optical drive and insert an optical disk. You can do the same thing on a virtual server by using the virtual machine settings. In addition, before you do any type of upgrade or major change, you can take a snapshot that can be used when something goes wrong during the upgrade or major change.
Completion time	10 minutes

1. On **WKSTN-MBR-B**, with *Hyper-V Manager* open from the previous exercise, right-click **VM1** and then click **Settings**. The *Settings for VM1* dialog box opens (see Figure 9-3).

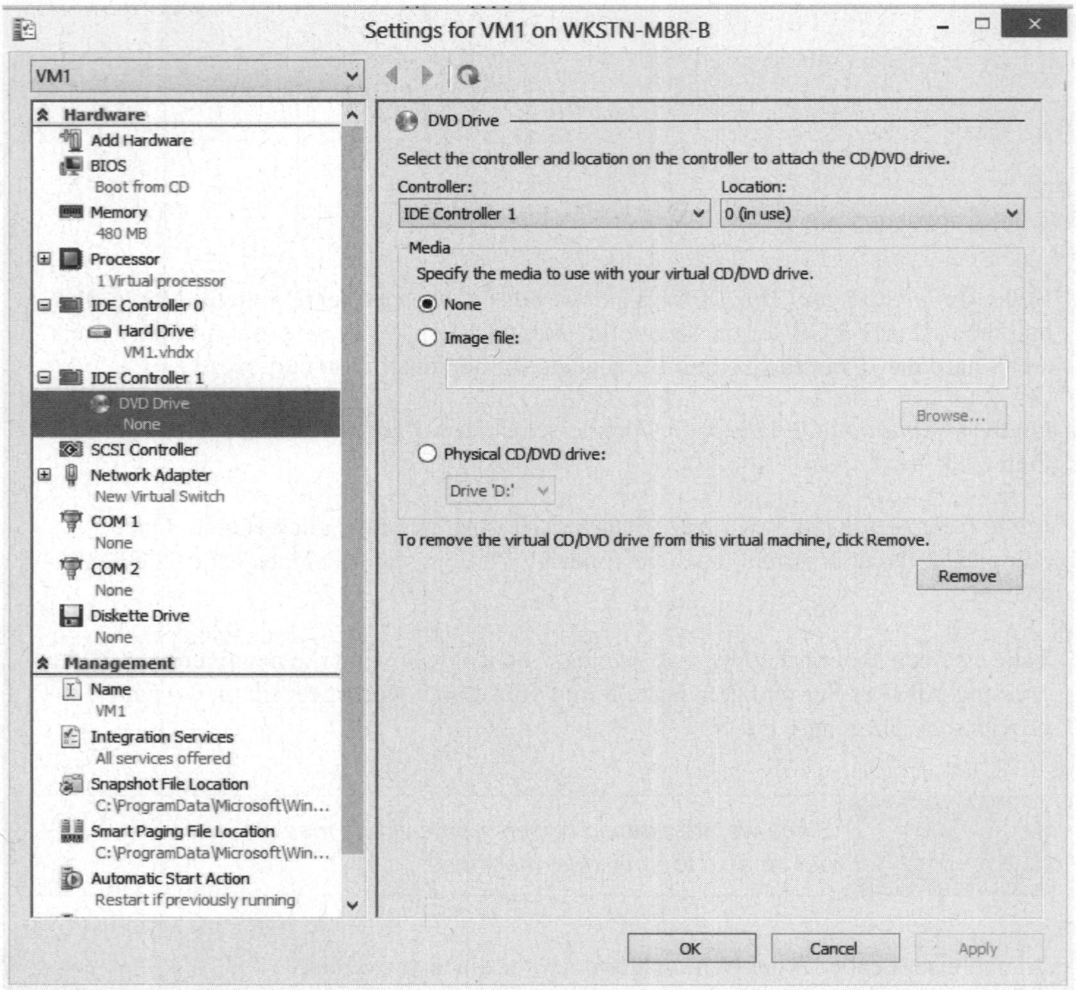

Figure 9-3
The VM settings dialog box

2. In the *Hardware* pane, under the *IDE Controller 1* section, click **DVD Drive**. On the right pane, click **Image file** and then click **Browse**.

3. In the *File name* text box, type **\\SVR-DC-A\Software**, click **Open**, and then double-click the Windows 8 image file.

4. Take a screen shot of the *Settings* window by pressing **Alt+Prt Scr** and then paste it into your Lab 9 worksheet file in the page provided by pressing **Ctrl+V**.

5. Click **OK** to close the *Settings* window.

6. To take a snapshot, right-click **VM1** and choose **Snapshot**.

Question 3	*What are snapshots used for?*

7. To delete the snapshot, right-click the **VM1** snapshot choose **Delete Snapshot**. When you are prompted to confirm if you want to delete the selected snapshot, click **Delete**.

End of exercise. Leave Hyper-V Manager open for the challenge lab.

Lab Challenge	Expanding a Virtual Hard Disk
Overview	In this challenge, you will expand the virtual hard drive for VM1 from 5 GB to 6 GB.
Mindset	As you install applications and add data files, you sometimes have to expand the drive.
Completion time	10 minutes

To complete this challenge, you have a virtual machine on your computer running Windows 8. Since the C drive is filling up, you need to first expand the C drive of the virtual machine from 5 GB to 6 GB. Write out the procedure to expand the drive and then take a snapshot of the *Expand Virtual Hard Disk* page by pressing **Alt+Prt Scr** and then paste the resulting image into the Lab 9 worksheet file in the page provided by pressing **Ctrl+V**.

End of lab.

LAB 10
CONFIGURING IP SETTINGS

THIS LAB CONTAINS THE FOLLOWING EXERCISES AND ACTIVITIES:

Exercise 10.1	Manually Configuring TCP/IP
Exercise 10.2	Creating and Managing a DHCP Scope
Exercise 10.3	Testing Network Connections
Lab Challenge	Configuring IP at the Command Prompt

BEFORE YOU BEGIN

The lab environment consists of student workstations connected to a local area network, along with a server that functions as the domain controller for a domain called adatum.com. The computers required for this lab are listed in Table 10-1.

Table 10-1
Computers Required for Lab 10

Computer	***Operating System***	***Computer Name***
Server	Windows Server 2012	SVR-DC-A
Client	Windows 8 Enterprise	WKSTN-MBR-B

In addition to the computers, you will also need the software listed in Table 10-2 to complete Lab 10.

Table 10-2
Software required for Lab 10

Software	*Location*
Lab 10 student worksheet	Lab10_worksheet.docx (provided by instructor)

Working with Lab Worksheets

Each lab in this manual requires that you answer questions, shoot screen shots, and perform other activities that you will document in a worksheet named for the lab, such as Lab10_worksheet.docx. You will find these worksheets on the book companion site. It is recommended that you use a USB flash drive to store your worksheets so you can submit them to your instructor for review. As you perform the exercises in each lab, open the appropriate worksheet file, type the required information, and then save the file to your flash drive.

SCENARIO

After completing this lab, you will be able to:

- Manually configure IPv4 Configuration on a computer running Windows 8
- Create and configure a DHCP scope
- Use basic IP configuration troubleshooting tools

Estimated lab time: 55 minutes

Exercise 10.1	Manually Configuring TCP/IP
Overview	In this exercise, you will configure the IP configuration of a computer running Windows 8.
Mindset	As an administrator, you will have to configure the IP settings for workstations and servers.
Completion time	20 minutes

1. On **WKSTN-MBR-B**, log on using the **adatum\Administrator** account and the **Pa$$w0rd** password. Click the Desktop tile.
2. Mouse over the lower-left corner of the desktop and right-click the **Start** screen thumbnail that appears there. Then, from the context menu that appears, click **Command Prompt (Admin)**.
3. When the command prompt displays, execute the following command:

```
ipconfig
```

Question 1	*What is the IPv4 address and subnet mask assigned to the computer?*

Question 2	*What is the IPv6 address?*

4. On the *Taskbar*, right-click the **Network Status** icon and choose **Open Network and Sharing Center**.

5. When the *Network and Sharing Center* window displays, click **Change adapter settings**.

6. Right-click the **Ethernet** adapter and choose **Properties**.

7. In the *Ethernet Properties* dialog box, scroll down and double-click **Internet Protocol Version 4 (TCP/IPv4)**.

8. In the *Internet Protocol Version 4 (TCP/IPv4) Properties* dialog box, click to select the **Obtain an IP address automatically** option and the **Obtain DNS server address automatically** option.

9. Click **OK** to close the *Internet Protocol Version 4 (TCP/IPv4) Properties* dialog box and then click **OK** to close the *Ethernet Properties* dialog box.

10. At the command prompt, execute the following command:

```
ipconfig /all
```

Question 3	*By looking at the response from ipconfig, what is the address of the DHCP server that assigned the IPv4 address to this computer?*

11. Close the *Command Prompt* window.

12. Back at the *Network Connections* window, right-click the **Ethernet connection** and choose **Status**.

13. In the *Ethernet Status* dialog box, click **Details**. This should display the same information you saw with the ipconfig /all command. Click **Close** to close the *Network Connection Details* dialog box.

14. In the *Ethernet Status* dialog box, click **Properties**.

15. In the *Ethernet Properties* dialog box (see Figure 10-1), scroll down and double-click **Internet Protocol Version 4 (TCP/IPv4)**.

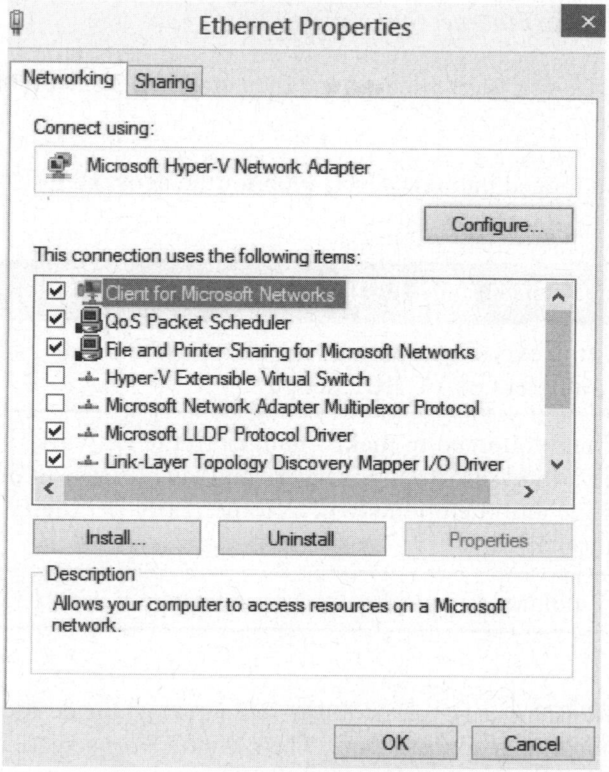

Figure 10-1
The *Ethernet Properties* dialog box

16. When the *Internet Protocol Version 4 (TCP/IPv4) Properties* dialog box displays, click **Use the following IP address**.

17. Type the following information:

    IP address: **10.0.0.2**

    Subnet mask: **255.255.255.0**

    Default gateway: **10.0.0.20**

18. Click to select the **Use the following DNS server addresses**.

19. For the *Preferred DNS server* setting, type **10.0.0.1**.

20. Take a screen shot of the *Internet Protocol Version 4 (TCP/IPv4) Properties* dialog box by pressing **Alt+Prt Scr** and then paste it into your Lab 10 worksheet file in the page provided by pressing **Ctrl+V**.

21. Click **OK** to close the *Internet Protocol Version 4 (TCP/IPv4) Properties* sheet.

22. Click **OK** to close the *Ethernet Properties* dialog box.

23. Click **Close** to close the *Ethernet Status* dialog box.

24. Close the *Network Connections* window and then close the *Network and Sharing Center* windows.

End of exercise. Remain logged into the workstation for the next exercise.

Exercise 10.2	Creating and Managing a DHCP Scope
Overview	In this exercise, you will create a DHCP scope and look at the parameters of a DHCP scope.
Mindset	When you need to make changes to the network, including changing the addresses of DNS servers and such, you can change the DHCP scope and the clients will automatically get the IP configuration automatically.
Completion time	15 minutes

1. On **WKSTN-MBR-B**, mouse over the lower-left corner of the desktop and click the **Start** screen thumbnail that appears there. Then, on the *Start* screen, click **Administrative Tools**.

2. Double-click **DHCP**.

3. When the *DHCP* console displays, right-click **DHCP** and choose **Add Server**.

4. In the *This server* text box, type **10.0.0.1** and then click **OK**.

5. Expand the **svr-dc-a node**, expand the **IPv4** node, and then expand the **Scope [10.0.0.0] Main Scope** node (see Figure 10-2).

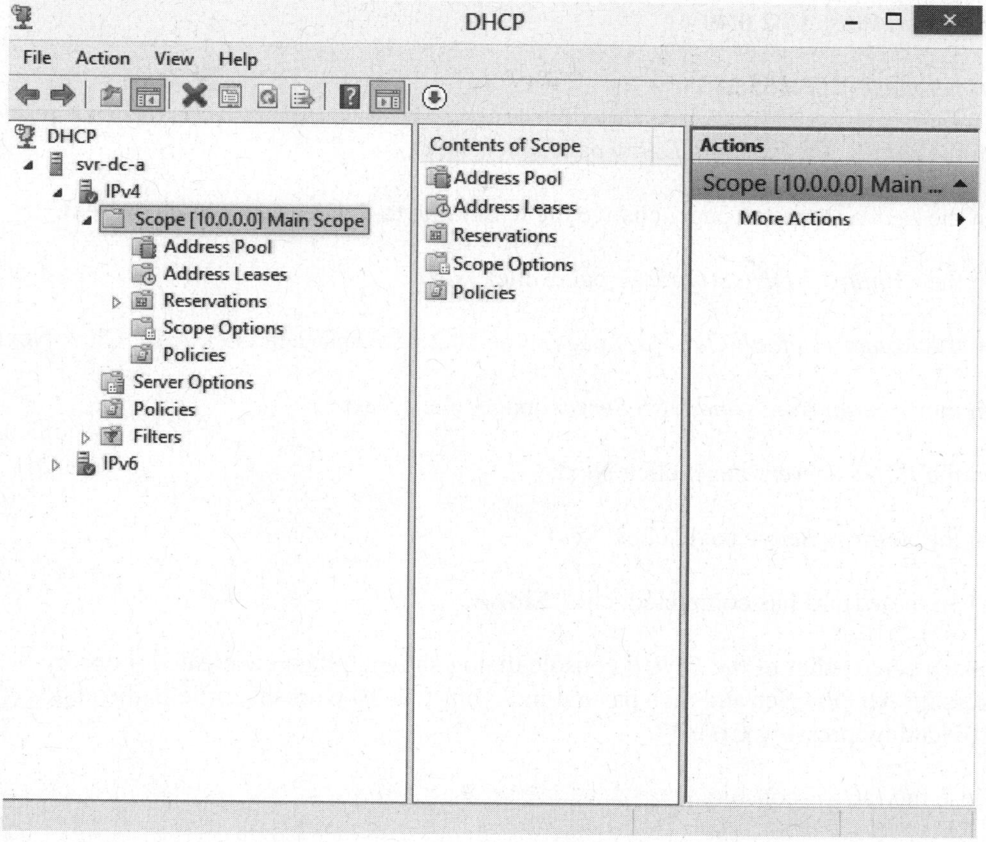

Figure 10-2
Expanding the *Scope* node

6. Right-click the **Scope [10.0.0.0] Main Scope** and choose **Properties**.

Question 4	*What is the start and end IP addresses being assigned?*

7. Click **OK** to close the *Scope [10.0.0.0] Main Scope Properties* dialog box.

8. Click **Address Leases** to view the current leases assigned.

9. To create a new DHCP scope, right-click **IPv4** and choose **New Scope**.

10. When the *New Scope* Wizard displays, click **Next**.

11. On the *Scope Name* page, in the *Name* text box, type **Test** and then click **Next**.

12. On the *IP Address Range* page, type the following information and then click **Next**:

    Start IP address: **10.2.0.30** —

End IP address: **10.2.0.40**

Subnet mask: **255.255.255.0**

13. On the *Add Exclusions and Delay* page, click **Next**.
14. On the *Lease Duration* page, change the lease time to **3** days and then click **Next**.
15. On the *Configure DHCP Options* page, click **Next**.
16. On the *Router (Default Gateway)* page, type **10.2.0.20** and then click **Add**. Click **Next**.
17. On the *Domain Name and DNS Servers* page, click **Next**.
18. On the *WINS Servers* page, click **Next**.
19. On the *Activate Scope* page, click **Next**.
20. When the wizard has completed, click **Finish**.
21. Take a screen shot of the *DHCP* console dialog showing the new created scope by pressing **Alt+Prt Scr** and then paste it into your Lab 10 worksheet file in the page provided by pressing **Ctrl+V**.
22. Close the *DHCP* console.

End of exercise. Leave the computer logged in for the next exercise.

Exercise 10.3	Testing Network Connections
Overview	In this exercise, you will test the network connection and network connectivity between computers. You will also use nslookup to get the IP address of a host.
Mindset	Network connection problems occur; they are usually caused by physical problems (such as when a cable is not connected) or by an IP configuration problem (such as having the wrong subnet mask or default gateway). As an administrator, you need to know how to troubleshoot such problems.
Completion time	10 minutes

1. On **WKSTN-MBR-B**, mouse over the lower-left corner of the desktop and right-click the **Start** screen thumbnail that appears there. Then, from the context menu that appears, click **Command Prompt (Admin)**.
2. At the command prompt, type **ping 127.0.0.1** (see Figure 10-3) and then press **Enter**.

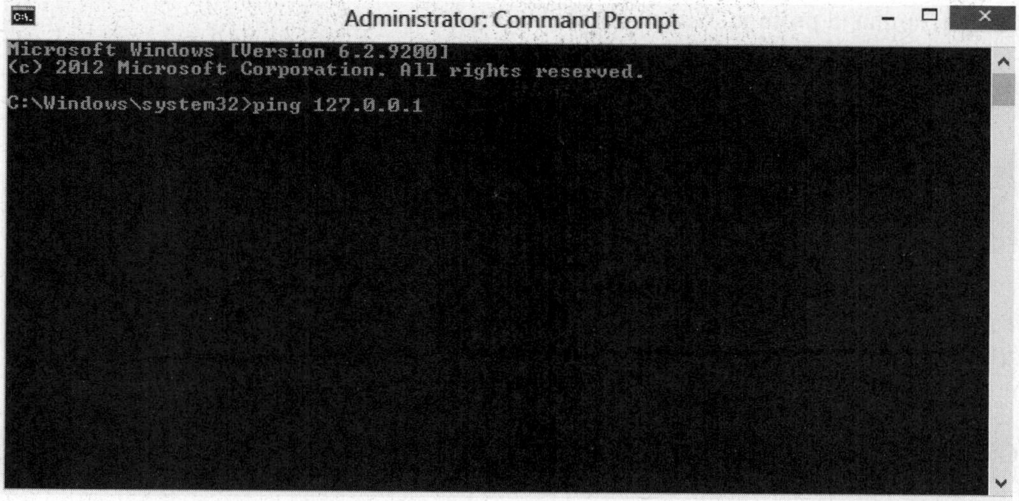

Figure 10-3
Executing the ping command

Question 5	*What is the result of executing ping 127.0.0.1?*

Question 6	*What does this result prove about the computer's network connectivity?*

Question 7	*What would be the result if you unplugged your computer's network cable before executing the ping 127.0.0.1 command?*

3. At the command prompt, type **ping SVR-DC-A** and then press **Enter**.

Question 8	*What is the result of executing ping SVR-DC-A and what does it prove?* Could not find host SVR-DC-A

Question 9	*What is the IP address of SVR-DC-A?*

4. At the command prompt, execute the following command:

   nslookup SVR-DC-A

Question 10	*What is the IP address of SVR-DC-A?*

5. Take a screen shot of the *Administrator Command Prompt* window by pressing **Alt+Prt Scr** and then paste it into your Lab 10 worksheet file in the page provided by pressing **Ctrl+V**.

6. Close the *Command Prompt* window.

End of exercise. Close any open windows before you begin the next exercise.

Lab Challenge	Configuring IP at the Command Prompt
Overview	In this exercise, you will perform a written exercise to demonstrate configuring IP settings using commands.
Mindset	As an administrator, you may want create scripts, which contain commands that you would execute to configure Windows. Some of these commands may include configuring IP.
Completion time	10 minutes

For this written exercise, answer the following questions.

1. Which command is used to configure the following?

   IP Address: 10.2.0.50

   Subnet mask: 255.255.255.0

   Default Gateway: 10.2.0.20

2. Which command is used to configure the primary DNS server as 10.0.0.50?
3. Which command would you set the computer to use DHCP?

End of lab.

LAB 11
CONFIGURING NETWORK SETTINGS

THIS LAB CONTAINS THE FOLLOWING EXERCISES AND ACTIVITIES:

Exercise 11.1 Configuring Network Adapter Settings

Lab Challenge Configuring Wireless Network Settings

BEFORE YOU BEGIN

The lab environment consists of student workstations connected to a local area network, along with a server that functions as the domain controller for a domain called adatum.com. The computers required for this lab are listed in Table 11-1.

Table 11-1
Computers Required for Lab 11

Computer	***Operating System***	***Computer Name***
Server	Windows Server 2012	SVR-DC-A
Client	Windows 8 Enterprise	WKSTN-MBR-B

In addition to the computers, you will also need the software listed in Table 11-2 to complete Lab 11.

Table 11-2
Software Required for Lab 11

Software	***Location***
Lab 11 student worksheet	Lab11_worksheet.docx (provided by instructor)

Working with Lab Worksheets

Each lab in this manual requires that you answer questions, shoot screen shots, and perform other activities that you will document in a worksheet named for the lab, such as Lab11_worksheet.docx. You will find these worksheets on the book companion site. It is recommended that you use a USB flash drive to store your worksheets so you can submit them to your instructor for review. As you perform the exercises in each lab, open the appropriate worksheet file, type the required information, and then save the file to your flash drive.

SCENARIO

After completing this lab, you will be able to:

- Configure network adapter settings
- Manage adapters using the Network Connections window

Estimated lab time: 40 minutes

Exercise 11.1	Configuring Network Adapter Settings
Overview	In this exercise, you will configure network adapters and their properties.
Mindset	While the common settings are configured directly using the Network and Sharing Center, you can configure additional settings using Network Connections window and the network adapter properties.
Completion time	20 minutes

1. On **WKSTN-MBR-B**, log on using the **adatum\administrator** account and the **Pa$$w0rd** password. Click the **Desktop** tile.
2. On the *Taskbar*, right-click the network connection icon and choose **Open Network and Sharing Center**.
3. In the *Network and Sharing Center* (see Figure 11-1), click **Change adapter settings**.

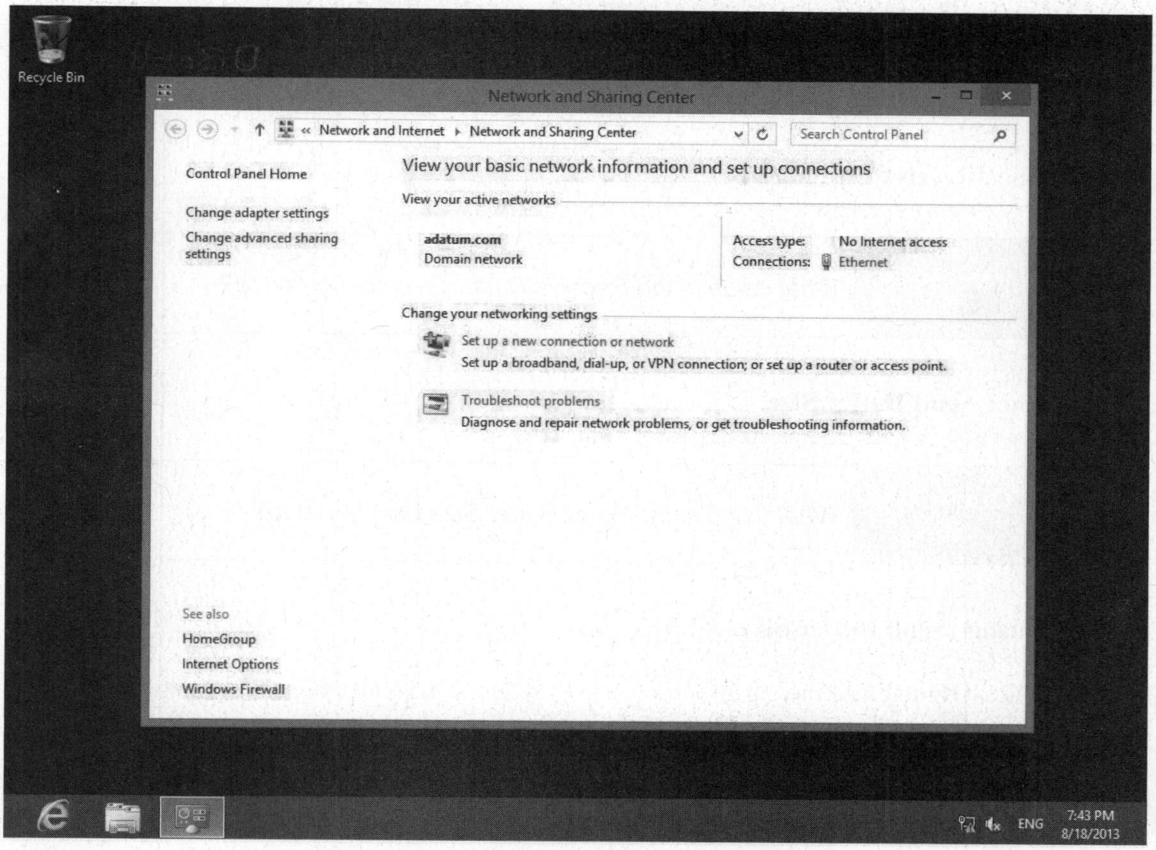

Figure 11-1
The *Network and Sharing Center*

4. In the *Network Connections* dialog box, right-click **Ethernet** and choose **Disable**.
5. With Ethernet already selected, click the **Enable this network device** button.
6. Right-click the **Ethernet** adapter and choose **Properties**. The Ethernet Properties dialog box opens.

Question 1	*What type of adapter is it the adapter using?*

7. Click the **Configure** button.
8. When the *Microsoft Hyper-V Network Adapter Properties* dialog box opens, click the **Advanced** tab.
9. Click **Jumbo Packet**.

Question 2	*What value is the Jumbo Packet configured to?* Disabled

10. Click **Receive Buffer Size**.

Question 3	*What value is the Receive Buffer Size configured to?* 256

11. Click **Send Buffer Size**.

Question 4	*What value is the Send Buffer Size configured to?*

12. Change **Send Buffer Size** to **2 MB**.
13. Click **OK** to close the *Microsoft Hyper-V Network Adapter Properties* dialog box.
14. The BCM5708C NetExtemeII GigE is an adapter that you may find on a physical computer, not on a virtual machine. Look at the *Broadcom BCM5708C NetXtreme II GigE* dialog box shown in Figure 11-2.

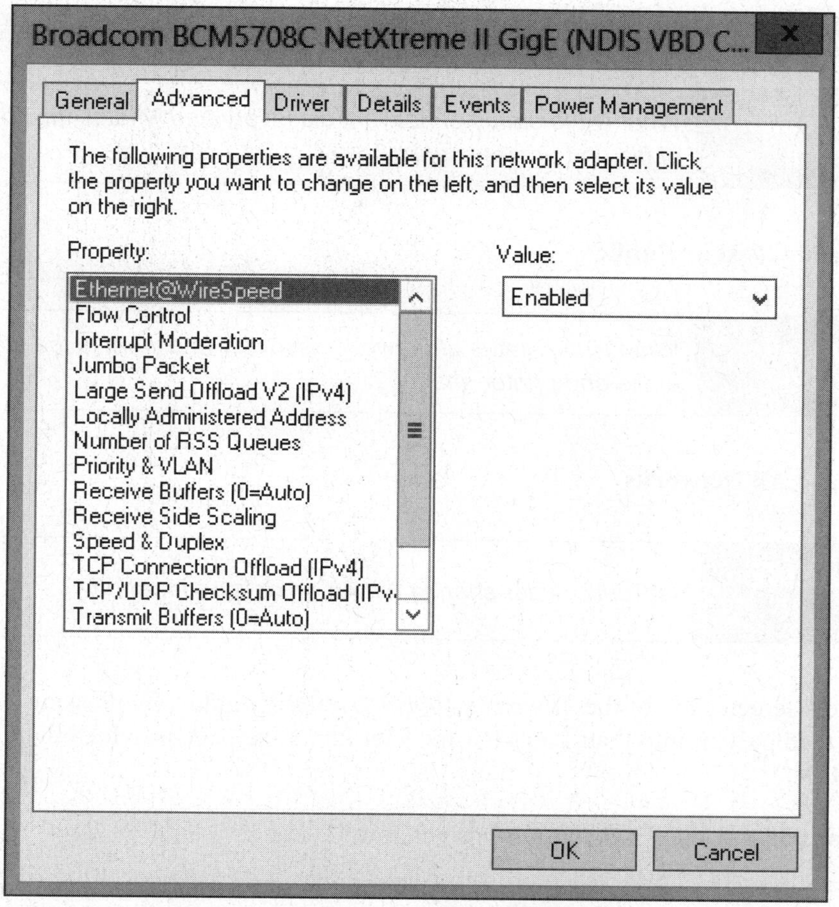

Figure 11-2
Broadcom adapter properties

Question 5	*You have a 1 Gbps adapter and you want to reduce the speed to 100 Mbps. Which settings would you select from Figure 11-2 to reduce the speed and which value would you select?*

15. In the *Network and Sharing Center* window, click **Change advanced sharing settings**.

Question 6	*What is the current profile?*

Question 7	*What is the status of network discovery and what is the status of file and printer sharing?*

16. Expand **Private**.

Question 8	*What is the status of network discovery and what is the status of file and printer sharing?*

17. Expand **Guest or Public**.

Question 9	*What is the status of network discovery and what is the status of file and printer sharing?*

18. Expand **All Networks**.

Question 10	*Is Public folder sharing turned on or is it turned off?*

19. Take a screen shot of the *Advanced sharing settings* window by pressing **Alt+Prt Scr** and then paste it into your Lab 11 worksheet file in the page provided by pressing **Ctrl+V**.

20. Close the *Advanced sharing settings* window.

Lab Challenge	Configuring Wireless Network Adapter Settings
Overview	In this lab challenge, you will identify the settings that are unique to wireless network adapters.
Mindset	Because the physical security capabilities of standard Ethernet networks do not apply, wireless networks must have additional security mechanisms.

To complete this challenge, specify how each of the following elements (see Figure 11-3 and Figure 11-4) contribute to the security of the network.

1. Connect even if the network is not broadcasting its name
2. Security type
3. Encryption type
4. Network security key

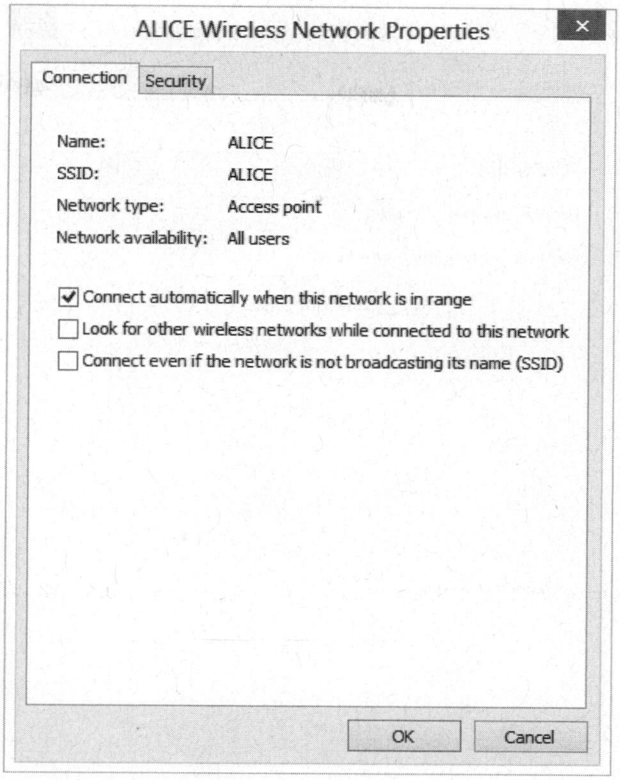

Figure 11-3
Wireless adapter properties

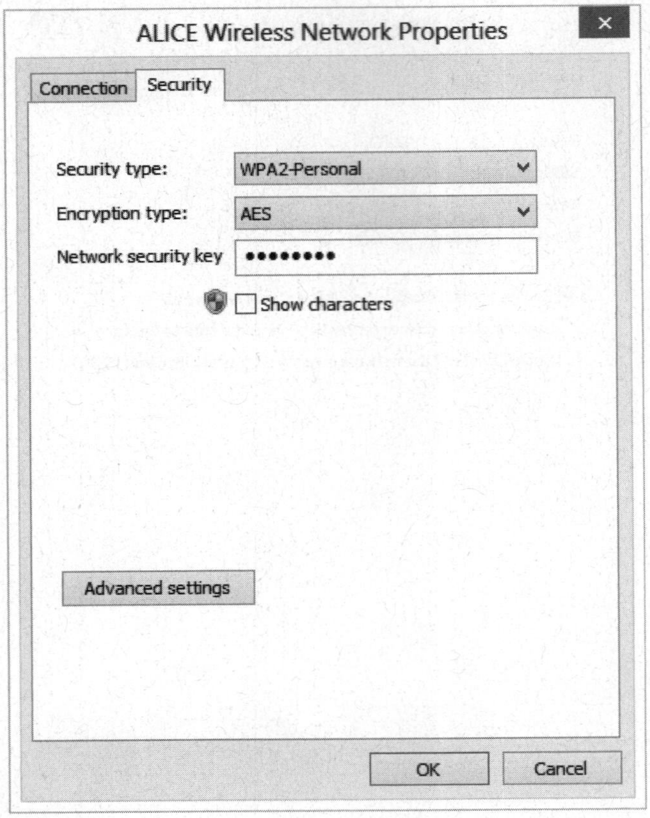

Figure 11-4
Wireless security properties

End of lab.

LAB 12
CONFIGURING AND MAINTAINING NETWORK SECURITY

THIS LAB CONTAINS THE FOLLOWING EXERCISES AND ACTIVITIES:

Exercise 12.1	Installing Internet Information Server
Exercise 12.2	Testing IIS Connectivity
Exercise 12.3	Allowing a Program Through the Firewall
Lab Challenge	Creating Windows Firewall Rules

BEFORE YOU BEGIN

The lab environment consists of computers connected to a local area network. The computers required for this lab are listed in Table 12-1.

Table 12-1
Computers Required for Lab 12

Computer	*Operating System*	*Computer Name*
Server	Windows Server 2012	SVR-DC-A
Workstation	Windows 8 Enterprise	WKSTN-MBR-B
Workstation	Windows 8 Enterprise	WKSTN-MBR-C

In addition to the computers, you will also need the software listed in Table 12-2 to complete Lab 12.

Table 12-2
Software Required for Lab 12

Software	***Location***
Lab 12 student worksheet	Lab12_worksheet.docx (provided by instructor)

Working with Lab Worksheets

Each lab in this manual requires that you answer questions, create screenshots, and perform other activities that you will document in a worksheet named for the lab, such as Lab12_worksheet.docx. You will find these worksheets on the book companion site. It is recommended that you use a USB flash drive to store your worksheets, so you can submit them to your instructor for review. As you perform the exercises in each lab, open the appropriate worksheet file, type the required information, and then save the file to your flash drive.

SCENARIO

After completing this lab, you will be able to:

- Configure Windows Firewall
- Create Windows Firewall rules

Estimated lab time: 60 minutes

Exercise 12.1	Installing Internet Information Server
Overview	Because this is only a test deployment, you will be using a Windows 8 computer to function as the web server. In this exercise, you will install Internet Information Services on your workstation and then configure it to host two websites.
Mindset	Internet Information Services enables you to configure websites to use specific port numbers. This makes it possible to test the functionality of Windows Firewall.
Completion time	15 minutes

1. On **WKSTN-MBR-B**, log on using the **adatum\Administrator** account and the **Pa$$w0rd** password.

2. On the *Start* screen, click the **Desktop** tile. The *Desktop* appears.

3. Mouse over the lower-right corner of the window and, when the Charms bar appears, click **Settings**.

4. On the *Settings* menu, click **Control Panel**. The *Control Panel* window appears.

5. Click **Programs > Programs and Features**. The *Uninstall or change a program* window appears.

6. Click **Turn Windows features on or off**. The *Windows Features* dialog box appears.

7. Browse to the *Internet Information Services\World Wide Web Services* folder, as shown in Figure 12-1.

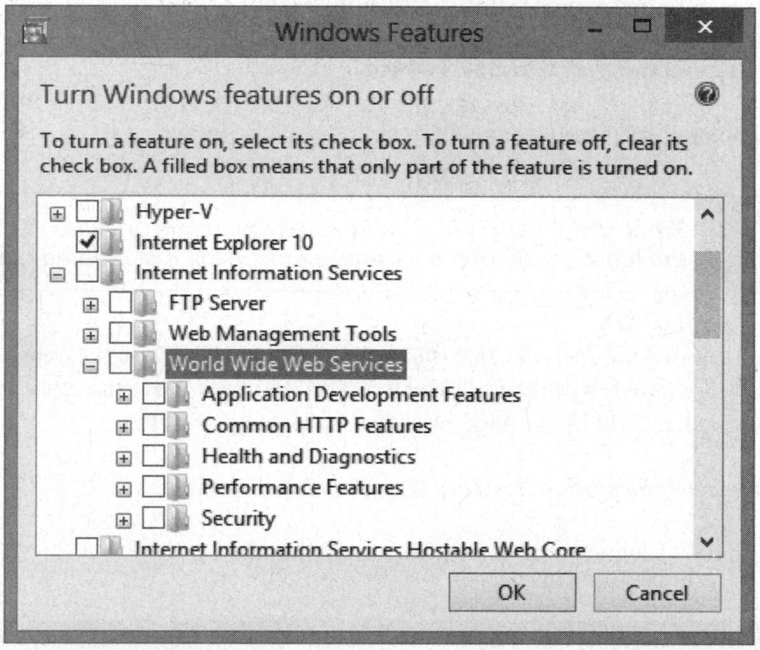

Figure 12-1
The World Wide Web Services folder in the *Windows Features* dialog box

8. Select the **Common HTTP Features** check box, the **Health and Diagnostics** check box, and the **Security** check box.

9. Expand the **Web Management Tools** folder, select the **IIS Management Console** check box, and then click **OK**. Windows 8 installs the selected components.

10. Close the **Windows Features** control panel window.

11. In the *Programs and Features* address bar, click **Control Panel** and then click **System and Security > Administrative Tools**. The *Administrative Tools* window appears.

12. Double-click **Internet Information Services (IIS) Manager**. The *Internet Information Services (IIS) Manager* console appears.

13. An *Internet Information Services (IIS) Manager* message box appears, prompting you to confirm if you want to stay connected.

14. Click **No**.

15. Expand the **WKSTN-MBR-B** container and then expand the **Sites** folder.

16. Right-click the **Sites** folder and, from the context menu, choose **Add Website**. The *Add Website* dialog box appears.

17. In the *Site* name text box, type **Intranet**.

18. In the *Physical* path text box, type **c:\inetpub\wwwroot**.

19. Change the value in the *Port* text box to **4444**.

20. Click **OK**. The new Intranet website appears in the *Sites* folder.

Question 1	*What URLs could you use in your computer's browser to test the functionality of the intranet website you just created?*

21. Take a screen shot of the *Internet Information Services (IIS) Manager* console, showing the new site you created, by pressing **Alt+Prt Scr**, and then paste the resulting image into the Lab 12 worksheet file in the page provided by pressing **Ctrl+V**.

22. Close the *Internet Information Services (IIS) Manager* console.

End of exercise. Leave all windows open for the next exercise.

Exercise 12.2	Testing IIS Connectivity
Overview	In this exercise, you will test the functionality of the web server you just installed.
Mindset	The way to test the functionality of a web server is to attempt to connect to it.
Completion time	15 minutes

1. On the **WKSTN-MBR-B** desktop, click the **Internet Explorer** button in the taskbar. An *Internet Explorer* window appears.

2. In the *Address* box, type **http://127.0.0.1** and then press **Enter**.

Question 2	*What is the result, and what does the result indicate?* Windows Internet explorer 10

3. Test the Intranet website by using the URLs you specified in Exercise 12-1, Question 1.

Question 3	*What is the result, and what does it indicate?*

4. On **WKSTN-MBR-C**, log on using the **adatum\Administrator** account and the **Pa$$w0rd** password.

5. Click the **Desktop** tile and then open **Internet Explorer**. Try to access the IIS web server running on your WKSTN-MBR-B workstation by typing **http://wkstn-mbr-b** in the *Address* box and pressing **Enter**.

Question 4	*What is the result?* This Page Can't be displayed

6. Now, try to connect to the Intranet website from **WKSTN-MBR-C**. C:\inetpub\wwwroot.

Question 5	*What is the result?* It openes wwwroot

Question 6	*List three possible reasons as to why you might be unable to connect to your computer's web server using a browser on another computer.*

7. Back on the **WKSTN-MBR-B** workstation, in the *System and Security* control panel, click **Windows Firewall**. The *Windows Firewall* control panel appears (see Figure 12-2).

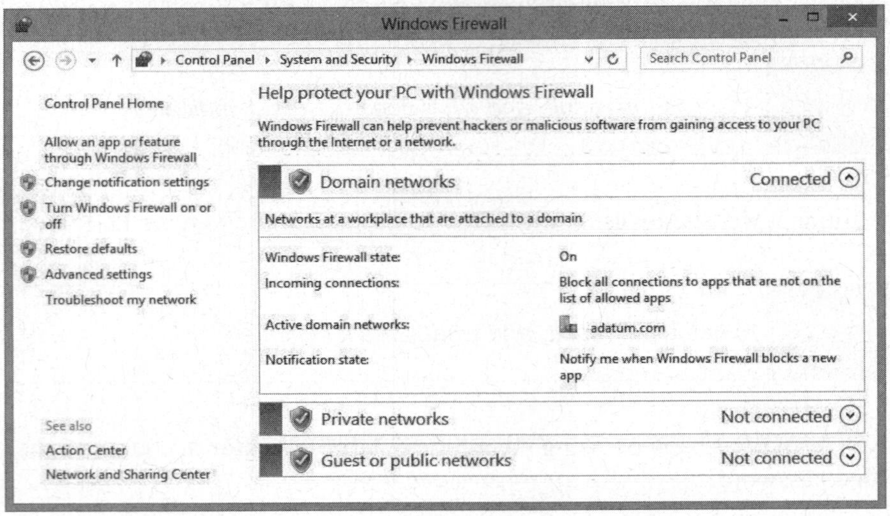

Figure 12-2
The Windows Firewall control panel

8. Below the *Control Panel Home* link on the left of the screen, click **Turn Windows Firewall on or off**. The *Customize settings for each type of network* window appears.

9. Under *Domain network settings*, select the **Turn off Windows Firewall (not recommended)** option.

10. Take a screen shot of the *Customize settings for each type of network* window, showing the setting you just modified, by pressing **Alt+Prt Scr**, and then paste the resulting image into the Lab 12 worksheet file in the page provided by pressing **Ctrl+V**. Click **OK**.

11. Back on **WKSTN-MBR-C**, try again to access both of the sites on the web server using Internet Explorer.

Question 7	*What are the results, and what do the results indicate?*

Question 8	*What other test could you perform to prove that it was your computer's firewall that was blocking the connection and not the firewall on the computer you are using as a client?*

12. Clear the Internet Explorer cache on **WKSTN-MBR-C** test client computer by clicking **Tools > Internet Options**. The *Internet Options* dialog box appears.

13. Under *Browsing History*, click the **Delete** button. The *Delete Browsing History* dialog box appears.

14. Click **Delete**. Then click **OK** to close the *Internet Options* dialog box.

Question 9	*Why is it necessary to clear the cache before you retest the web server connections?*

15. Back on **WKSTN-MBR-B**, in the *Windows Firewall* control panel, click **Turn Windows Firewall on or off** to open the *Customize settings for each type of network* window again, and then turn the **Domain network settings** Windows Firewall back on. Click **OK** to close the window.

Question 10	*Why can you not simply leave Windows Firewall turned off when you deploy an actual web server?*

End of exercise. Leave all windows open for the next exercise.

Exercise 12.3	Allowing a Program Through the Firewall
Overview	Windows Firewall is preventing clients from connecting to your web server. To enable client access, you will use the Windows Firewall control panel to allow access to the web server.
Mindset	The Windows Firewall control panel provides access to basic functions of the firewall, but for complete control, you must use the Windows Firewall with Advanced Security console, which you'll see in the Lab Challenge.
Completion time	10 minutes

1. On **WKSTN-MBR-B**, in the *Windows Firewall* control panel, click **Allow an app or feature through Windows Firewall**. The *Allow apps to communicate through Windows Firewall* window appears (see Figure 12-3).

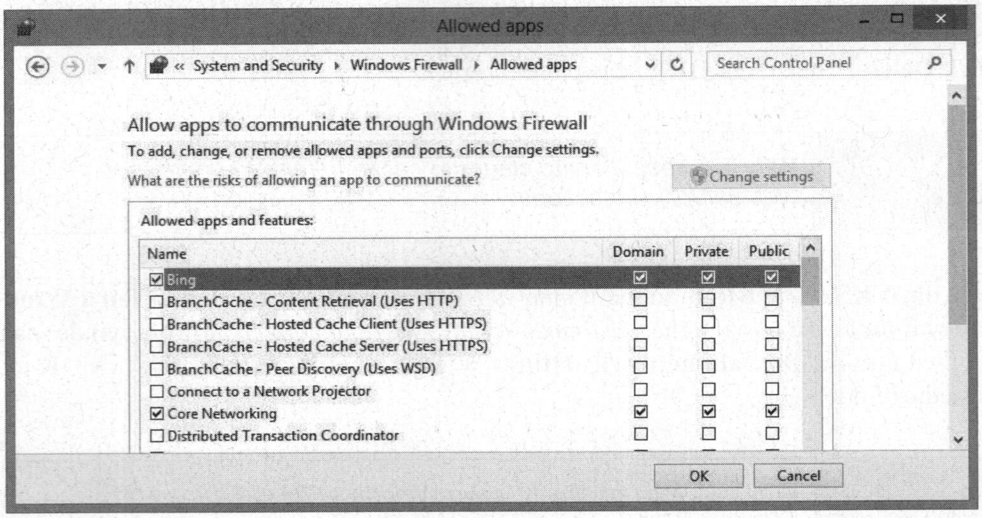

Figure 12-3
The *Allow apps to communicate through Windows Firewall* window

2. Scroll down the *Allowed apps and features* list and, in the *Domain* column, select the **World Wide Web Services (HTTP)** check box and then click **OK**.

3. On **WKSTN-MBR-C**, try again to connect to the default website at **http://wkstn-mbr-b**.

Question 11	*Why are you now able to connect to the website from the client?*

4. Now, try to connect to the Intranet website.

Question 12	*Why are you unable to connect to the intranet site from the client?*

5. On **WKSTN-MBR-B**, open the **Allow an app or feature through Windows Firewall** window again and clear the **World Wide Web Services (HTTP)** check box. Then click **OK**.

End of exercise. Leave all windows open for the next exercise.

Lab Challenge	Creating Windows Firewall Rules
Overview	The port you opened in Exercise 12.3 enables clients to access the default website hosted by your web server, but not the Intranet website. In this challenge, you must configure your web server to allow traffic to the Intranet website.
Mindset	Windows 8 often provides more than one way to complete a given task. The Windows Firewall control panel provides a relatively simple interface to the firewall, but it is not a comprehensive one, as we saw in the previous Exercise.
Completion time	20 minutes

To complete this challenge, you must use the Windows Firewall With Advanced Security console to configure WKSTN-MBR-B to allow traffic to both the default website and the Intranet website you created in Exercise 12.1.

To complete the challenge, perform the following tasks:

1. List the steps you took to complete the task.
2. Take a screen shot of the interface you used to create the firewall rules by pressing **Alt+Prt Scr** and then paste it into your Lab 12 worksheet file in the page provided by pressing **Ctrl+V**.
3. Answer the following questions.

Question 13	*Why are there two separate rules for the World Wide Web Services in the Inbound Rules container?*

Question 14	*How would the opening of the port you performed in Exercise 12.3 affect the World Wide Web Services (HTTP Traffic-In) rules in the Inbound Rules container?*

Question 15	*How would the rule creation procedure you just performed differ if you wanted to restrict client access to the intranet website to computers on the local network only?*

End of lab.

LAB 13
CONFIGURING REMOTE MANAGEMENT

THIS LAB CONTAINS THE FOLLOWING EXERCISES AND ACTIVITIES:

Exercise 13.1	Configuring Remote Desktop Client
Exercise 13.2	Connecting to a Remote Workstation
Lab Exercise	Using Windows Remote Management

BEFORE YOU BEGIN

The lab environment consists of computers connected to a local area network. The computers required for this lab are listed in Table 13-1.

Table 13-1
Computers Required for Lab 13

Computer	*Operating System*	*Computer Name*
Server	Windows Server 2012	SVR-DC-A
Workstation	Windows 8 Enterprise	WKSTN-MBR-B
Workstation	Windows 8 Enterprise	WKSTN-MBR-C

In addition to the computers, you will also need the software listed in Table 13-2 to complete Lab 13.

Table 13-2
Software Required for Lab 13

Software	*Location*
Lab 13 student worksheet	Lab13_worksheet.docx (provided by instructor)

Working with Lab Worksheets

Each lab in this manual requires that you answer questions, create screenshots, and perform other activities that you will document in a worksheet named for the lab, such as Lab13_worksheet.docx. You will find these worksheets on the book companion site. It is recommended that you use a USB flash drive to store your worksheets so you can submit them to your instructor for review. As you perform the exercises in each lab, open the appropriate worksheet file, type the required information, and then save the file to your flash drive.

SCENARIO

After completing this lab, you will be able to:

- Configure Remote Desktop Client
- Connect to another system using Remote Desktop Client

Estimated lab time: 35 minutes

Exercise 13.1	Configuring Remote Desktop Client
Overview	Before you can test the Remote Desktop Client program, both of the Windows 8 computers involved must be configured to allow secured connections to occur. In this exercise, you will configure the Remote Access settings on your workstations.
Mindset	By default, Windows 8 disables the operating system's ability to receive incoming Remote Desktop client requests.
Completion time	10 minutes

1. On **WKSTN-MBR-B**, log on using the **adatum\Administrator** account and the **Pa$$w0rd** password.

2. On the *Start* page, type **Control Panel**.

3. Click the **Control Panel** tile. The *Control Panel* window appears.

4. Click **System and Security** > **System**. The *System* control panel appears.

5. Click **Remote settings**. The *System Properties* sheet appears with the Remote tab selected (see Figure 13-1).

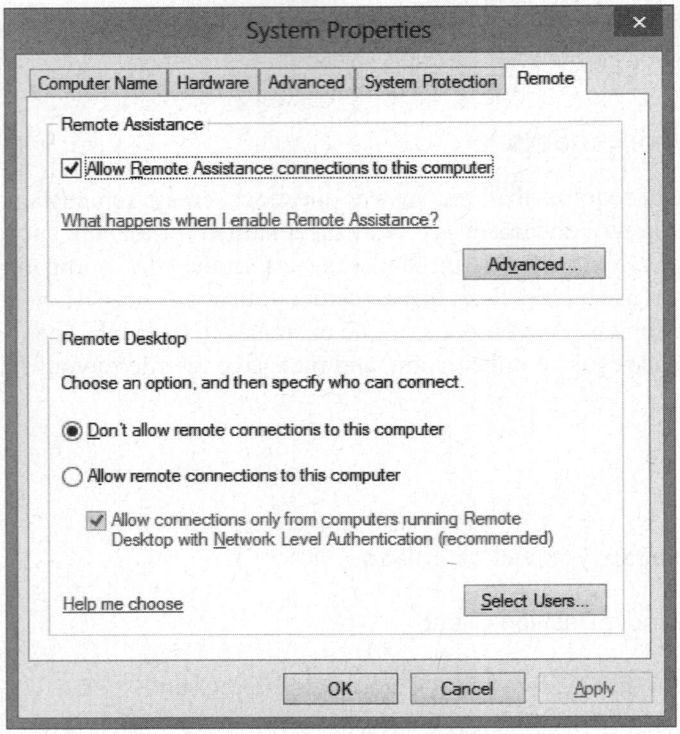

Figure 13-1
The *System Properties* sheet

6. Leave the **Allow Remote Assistance connections to this computer** check box selected and, in the Remote Desktop area, select the **Allow remote connections to this computer** option and then click **Advanced**. The *Remote Assistance Settings* dialog box appears.

7. Make sure that the **Allow this computer to be controlled remotely** check box is selected and then configure **Set the maximum amount of time invitations can remain open** to **24 Hours** (see Figure 13-2).

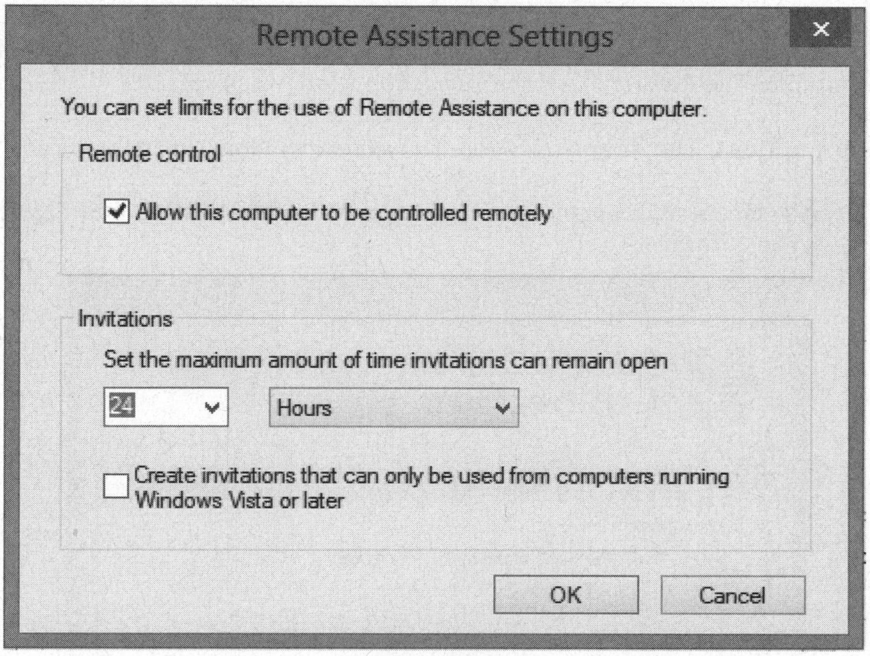

Figure 13-2
The *Remote Assistance Settings* sheet

8. Click **OK**.

Question 1	*When using Remote Assistance, why might it be necessary to impose a time limit on the invitation?*

9. Click **OK** to close the *System Properties* dialog box.

End of exercise. Close all windows and log off of the computer.

Exercise 13.2	Connecting to a Remote Workstation
Overview	In this exercise, you will connect to another computer and control it from a remote location.
Mindset	The Remote Desktop feature in Windows 8 does not require a user to be present at the remote computer.
Completion time	15 minutes

1. On **WKSTN-MBR-C**, log on using the **adatum\Administrator** account and the **Pa$$w0rd** password.

2. Mouse over the lower-right corner of the window and, when the Charms bar appears, click **Search**.

3. In the *Search* box, type **Remote** and, in the results list, click the **Remote Desktop Connection** tile. The *Remote Desktop Connection* window appears.

4. Click **Show options**. The *Remote Desktop Connection* window expands.

5. On the *General* tab, in the *Computer* text box, type **WKSTN-MBR-B** (see Figure 13-3).

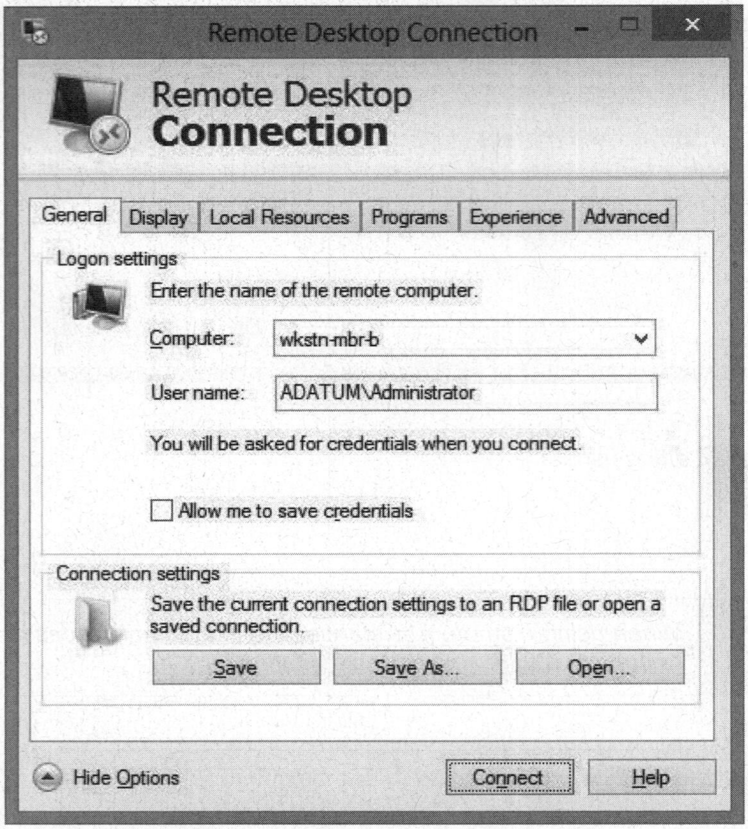

Figure 13-3
The expanded *Remote Desktop Connection* window

6. Click the **Display** tab.

7. Set the **Display Configuration** slider to **800 by 600** pixels.

8. Click the **Local Resources** tab.

9. Clear the **Printers** check box and then click **More**. The *Local devices and resources* dialog box appears.

10. Select the **Drives** check box and then click **OK**.

11. Click the **Experience** tab.

12. From the *Choose your connection speed to optimize performance* drop-down list, select **LAN (10 Mbps or Higher)**.

13. Click **Connect**. A *Remote Desktop Connection* message box appears, prompting you to confirm that you trust the remote computer.

14. Select the *Don't ask me again for connections to this computer* check box and then click **Connect**.

15. Type the **Pa$$w0rd** password for the **adatum\Administrator** account and then click **OK**.

16. A *WKSTN-MBR-B — Remote Desktop Connection* window appears, showing an image of the remote computer's desktop.

17. Take a screen shot of the *WKSTN-MBR-B — Remote Desktop Connection* window by pressing **Alt+Prt Scr** and then paste the resulting image into the Lab 13 worksheet file in the page provided by pressing **Ctrl+V**.

18. In the *WKSTN-MBR-B — Remote Desktop Connection* window, mouse over the lower-right corner of the window and, when the Charms bar appears, click **Search**.

19. In the *Search* box, type **Notepad**. In the results list, click the **Notepad** tile. The *Notepad* window appears.

Question 2	*On which computer is the Notepad program actually running?*

20. In the *Notepad* window, click **File > Open**. The *Open* combo box appears.

Question 3	*When you browse the Local Disk (C:) drive in the Open combo box, which computer's C: drive are you actually looking at?*

21. In the *Open* combo box, select the **Computer** container and then scroll down to display the **WKSTN-MBR-C** disks.

22. Take a screen shot of the *WKSTN-MBR-B — Remote Desktop Connection* window, showing the *WKSTN-MBR-C* disks in the *Open* combo box, by pressing **Alt+Prt Scr** and then paste the resulting image into the Lab 13 worksheet file in the page provided by pressing **Ctrl+V**.

Question 4	*Why Is it possible to access the host computer's – that is, the WKSTN-MBR-C computer's – various drives while working in the WKSTN-MBR-B Remote Desktop Connection window?*

23. Click **Cancel** to close the *Open* combo box.

Question 5	*During a Remote Desktop session, what would happen if you opened the Network Connections window on the remote computer and configured the network adapter to use a different IP address? Explain the result.*

24. Close the *Notepad* window.

25. Close the *WKSTN-MBR-B — Remote Desktop Connection* window. A *Remote Desktop Connection* message box appears, informing you that this will disconnect the Remote Desktop session.

26. Click **OK**. The *WKSTN-MBR-B — Remote Desktop Connection* window closes.

End of exercise. Close all windows and log off of the computer.

Lab Challenge	Using Windows Remote Management
Overview	In this exercise, you will configure a Windows 8 workstation to accept commands issued remotely from other computers.
Mindset	Windows Remote Management is a service that enables administrators to execute command-line programs on a remote computer by running a remote shell program called Winrs.exe.
Completion time	10 minutes

To complete this challenge, you must write out the complete procedure for enabling Windows Remote Management and executing a command that uses the adatum\Administrator account to create a local user account for a user called Mark Lee (**mlee**) with the **Pa$$w0rd** password on the remote workstation. After writing out the procedure, execute it on your workstation and take a screen shot showing the creation of the user account.

End of lab.

LAB 14
CONFIGURING SHARED RESOURCES

THIS LAB CONTAINS THE FOLLOWING EXERCISES AND ACTIVITIES:

Exercise 14.1	Sharing a Folder
Exercise 14.2	Sharing a Printer
Lab Challenge	Creating a Homegroup

BEFORE YOU BEGIN

The lab environment consists of computers connected to a local area network in a workgroup configuration. The computers required for this lab are listed in Table 14-1.

Table 14-1
Computers Required for Lab 14

Computer	*Operating System*	*Computer Name*
Server	Windows Server 2012	SVR-WKGRP-A
Workstation	Windows 8 Enterprise	WKSTN-WKGRP-B
Workstation	Windows 8 Enterprise	WKSTN-WKGRP-C

In addition to the computers, you will also need the software listed in Table 14-2 to complete Lab 14.

Table 14-2
Software Required for Lab 14

Software	***Location***
Lab 14 student worksheet	Lab14_worksheet.docx (provided by instructor)

Working with Lab Worksheets

Each lab in this manual requires that you answer questions, create screenshots, and perform other activities that you will document in a worksheet named for the lab, such as Lab14_worksheet.docx. You will find these worksheets on the book companion site. It is recommended that you use a USB flash drive to store your worksheets so you can submit them to your instructor for review. As you perform the exercises in each lab, open the appropriate worksheet file, type the required information, and then save the file to your flash drive.

SCENARIO

After completing this lab, you will be able to:

- Share folders and printers
- Create a homegroup

Estimated lab time: 60 minutes

Exercise 14.1	Sharing a Folder
Overview	In this exercise, you will share a folder on a Windows 8 workstation and control access to it using share permissions.
Mindset	Share permissions enable you to control access to shared resources, but only when users access the resources over the network.
Completion time	20 minutes

1. On **WKSTN-WKGRP-B**, log on using the **wkstn-wrkgrp-b\ocox** account and the **Pa$$w0rd** password.
2. On the Start screen, click the **Desktop** tile. The *Desktop* appears.
3. On the Taskbar, click the **File Explorer** icon. The *File Explorer* window appears.
4. Browse to the *C:\Users\ocox* folder.
5. Right-click the **My Documents** folder and choose **Properties**. The *My Documents Properties* sheet appears.

6. Click the **Sharing** tab and then click **Advanced Sharing**. The *Advanced Sharing* dialog box appears (see Figure 14-1).

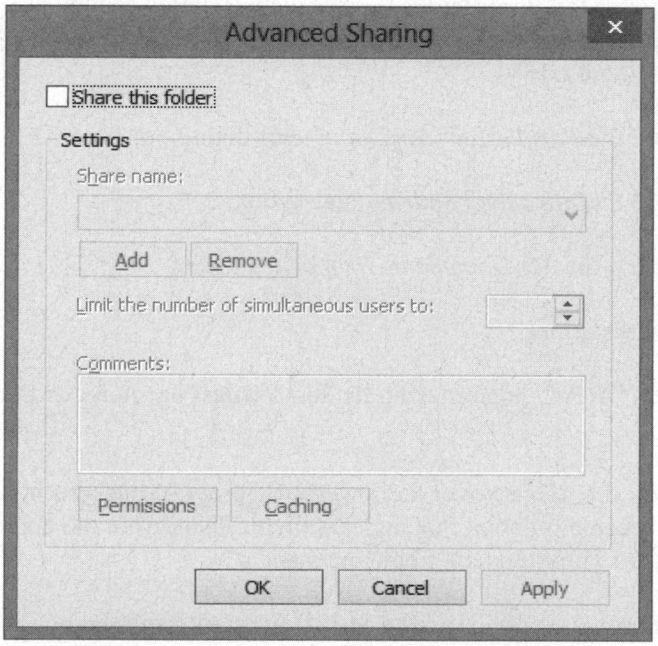

Figure 14-1
The Advanced Sharing dialog box

7. Select the **Share this folder** check box. The *Documents* default value appears in the *Share name* text box.

8. Click **Permissions**. The *Permissions for Documents* dialog box appears.

9. Select the **Everyone** special identity and, in the *Allow* column, clear all of the check boxes.

10. Click **Add**. The *Select Users or Groups* dialog box appears.

11. In the *Enter the object names to select* box, type **Administrators** and then click **OK**. The Administrators group appears in the *Group or user names* list in the *Permissions for Documents* dialog box.

12. Select the **Administrators** group and then, in the *Permissions for Administrators* box, in the *Allow* column, select the **Full Control** check box. This action also selects the **Change** check box.

13. Using the same technique, add the **Users** group to the *Group or user names* list and then assign it the **Allow Change** permission and **Allow Read** permission.

14. In the *Group or user names* list, add the **Guest** user account to and then assign it the **Allow Read** permission only.

15. Take a screen shot of the *Permissions for Documents* dialog box by pressing **Alt+Prt Scr**, and then paste the resulting image into the Lab 14 worksheet file in the page provided by pressing **Ctrl+V**.

16. Click **OK** to close the *Permissions for Documents* dialog box.

17. Click **OK** to close the *Advanced Sharing* dialog box.

18. Click **Close** to close the *My Documents Properties* sheet.

19. Log off of the workstation.

20. On **WKSTN-WKGRP-C**, log on using the local **Guest** account and the **Pa$$w0rd** password.

21. Click the **Desktop** tile, mouse over the lower-left corner of the screen, and then right-click the **Start** screen thumbnail that appears there. Then, from the context menu that appears, click **Run**. The *Run* dialog box appears.

22. In the *Open* text box, type **\\wkstn-wkgrp-b\Documents** and then click **OK**. A Network Error window appears, informing you that you do not have permission to access *\\wkstn-wkgrp-b\Documents*.

23. Take a screen shot of the *Network Error* window by pressing **Alt+Prt Scr**, and then paste the resulting image into the Lab 14 worksheet file in the page provided by pressing **Ctrl+V**.

Question 1	*Why are you unable to access the share using the Guest account, despite having granted the user the Allow Read permission?*

Question 2	*Would the Guest user be able to access the share if you granted it the Allow Full Control share permission, rather than the Allow Read permission?*

24. Log off **WKSTN-WKGRP-C** and then log on again using the **wkstn-wkgrp-c\ocox** account and the **Pa$$w0rd** password.

25. Click the **Desktop** tile, mouse over the lower-left corner of the desktop, and then right-click the **Start** screen thumbnail that appears there. Then, from the context menu that appears, click **Run**. The *Run* dialog box appears.

26. In the *Open* text box, type **wkstn-wkgrp-b\Documents** and then click **OK**. An *Explorer* window appears, displaying the contents of the support folder.

Question 3	*Why are you able to access the share, despite having logged on using the ocox account on WKSTN-WKGRP-C, not WKSTN-WKGRP-B?*

End of exercise. Close any open windows before you begin the next exercise.

Exercise 14.2	Sharing a Printer
Overview	In this exercise, you will create a new printer and share it with network users.
Mindset	Printers have a separate system of shares and share permissions that enable you to control access to the physical print device.
Completion time	20 minutes

1. On **WKSTN-MBR-B**, log on using the **wkstn-wrkgrp-b\ocox** account and the **Pa$$w0rd** password.

2. On the Start screen, click the **Desktop** tile. The Desktop appears.

3. Mouse over the lower-left corner of the desktop and right-click the **Start** screen thumbnail that appears there. Then, from the context menu that appears, click **Control Panel**. The *Control Panel* appears.

4. Click **Hardware and Sound > Devices and Printers**. The *Devices and Printers* control panel appears (see Figure 14-2).

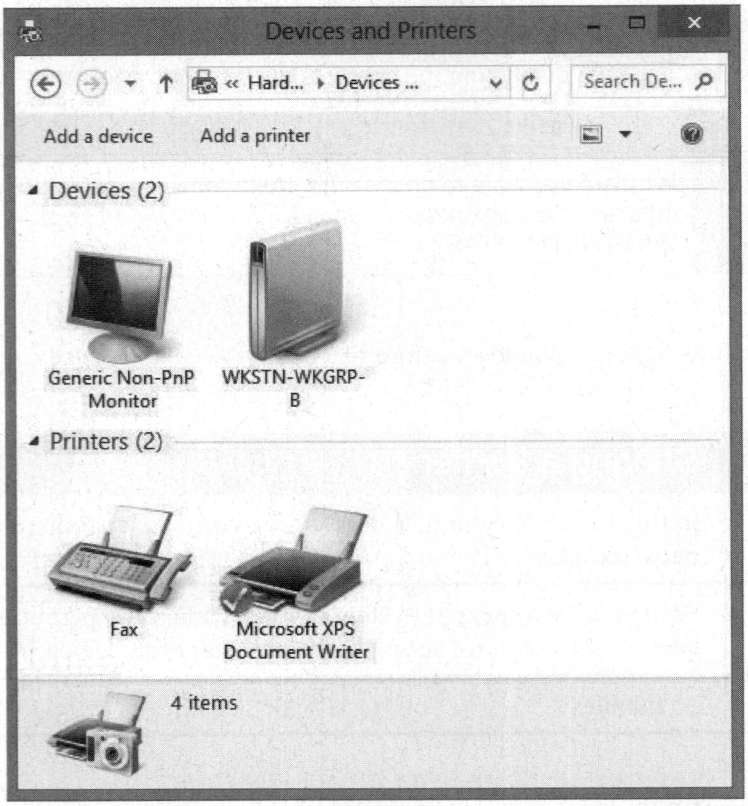

Figure 14-2
The Devices and Printers control panel

5. Click **Add a printer**. The *Add Printer Wizard* appears and searches for attached print devices. When it finds none, a *No printers were found* message appears.

6. Click **The printer that I want isn't listed**. The *Find a printer by other options* page appears.

7. Select **Add a local printer or network printer with manual settings** and then click **Next**. The *Choose a printer port* page appears.

8. Leaving the **Use an existing port** option selected, click **LPT2: (Printer Port)** from the drop-down list and then click **Next**. The *Install the printer driver* page appears.

Question 4	*Why doesn't Windows 8 attempt to automatically detect a printer connected to the computer?*

9. In the *Manufacturer* column, click **Generic**. In the *Printers* column, click **MS Publisher Color Printer** and then click **Next**. The *Type a printer name* page appears.

10. In the *Printer Name* text box, type **MS Color** and then click **Next**. The wizard installs the driver and the *Printer Sharing* page appears.

11. Select the *Do not share this printer* option and then click **Next**. The *You've Successfully Added MS Color* page appears.

12. Click **Finish**. The *MS Color* icon appears in the *Devices and Printers* control panel.

13. Take a screen shot of the *Devices and Printers* control panel displaying the new printer icon you created by pressing **Alt+Prt Scr**, and then paste the resulting image into the Lab 14 worksheet file in the page provided by pressing **Ctrl+V**.

14. Right-click the **MS Color** icon and choose **Printer properties**. The *MS Color Properties* sheet appears.

15. Click the **Sharing** tab (see Figure 14-3).

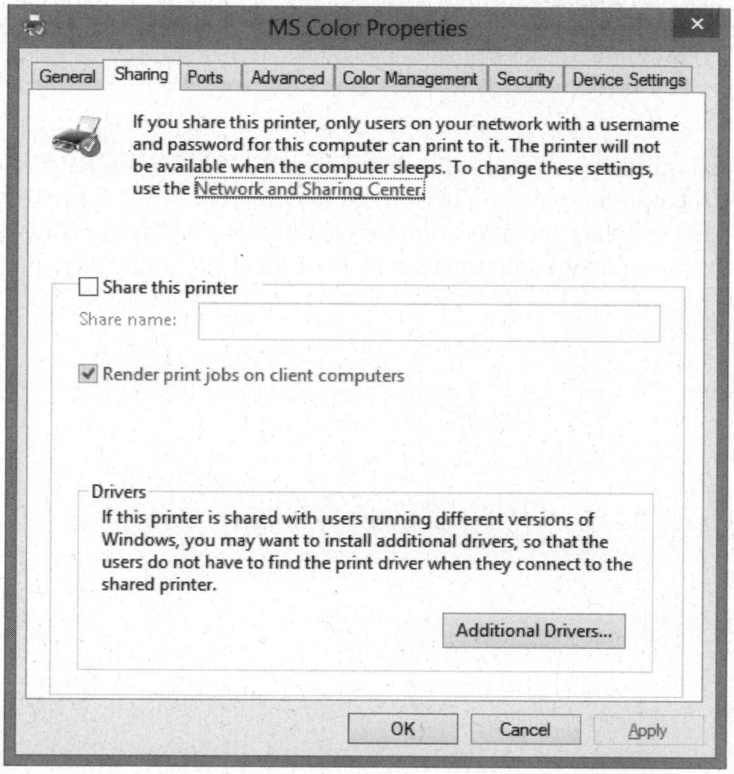

Figure 14-3
The Sharing tab of a printer's Properties sheet

16. Select the **Share this printer** check box. Leave the **Render print jobs on client computers** check box selected and then click **OK**.

Question 5	*How can you tell whether the printer has been shared?*

End of exercise. Close any open windows before you begin the next exercise.

Lab Challenge	Creating a Homegroup
Overview	Homegroup networking is a Windows 8 feature that enables computers configured to use the Private network location to share the contents of their respective libraries among themselves.
Mindset	Homegroups simplify the process of sharing files among workgroup network users.
Completion time	20 minutes

In this challenge, you must create a homegroup and join WKSTN-WKGRP-B and WKSTN-WKGRP-C to it. Write out the steps you performed to complete these tasks. Then take a screen shot of the page showing the password for your homegroup by pressing **Alt+Prt Scr** and then paste the resulting image into the Lab 14 worksheet file in the page provided by pressing **Ctrl+V**.

End of lab.

LAB 15
CONFIGURING FILE AND FOLDER ACCESS

THIS LAB CONTAINS THE FOLLOWING EXERCISES AND ACTIVITIES:

Exercise 15.1	Configuring NTFS Permissions
Exercise 15.2	Configuring NTFS Quotas
Exercise 15.3	Configuring Auditing
Lab Challenge	Viewing Audit Data

BEFORE YOU BEGIN

The lab environment consists of computers connected to a local area network. The computers required for this lab are listed in Table 15-1.

Table 15-1
Computers Required for Lab 15

Computer	*Operating System*	*Computer Name*
Server	Windows Server 2012	SVR-DC-A
Workstation	Windows 8 Enterprise	WKSTN-MBR-B
Workstation	Windows 8 Enterprise	WKSTN-MBR-C

In addition to the computers, you will also require the software listed in Table 15-2 to complete Lab 15.

Table 15-2
Software Required for Lab 15

Software	***Location***
Lab 15 student worksheet	Lab15_worksheet.docx (provided by instructor)

Working with Lab Worksheets

Each lab in this manual requires that you answer questions, create screenshots, and perform other activities that you will document in a worksheet named for the lab, such as Lab15_worksheet.docx. You will find these worksheets on the book companion site. It is recommended that you use a USB flash drive to store your worksheets so you can submit them to your instructor for review. As you perform the exercises in each lab, open the appropriate worksheet file, type the required information, and then save the file to your flash drive.

SCENARIO

After completing this lab, you will be able to:

- Configure NTFS permissions and quotas
- Configure Auditing
- Audit Windows activities

Estimated lab time: 60 minutes

Exercise 15.1	Configuring NTFS Permissions
Overview	To enable users to access the files on a Windows 8 computer, they must have the appropriate NTFS permissions. In this exercise, you will configure the permissions to enable the Student user to access a shared folder.
Mindset	Users need NTFS permissions to access files on an NTFS disk, whether they are sitting at the console or accessing the disk over the network.
Completion time	20 minutes

1. On **WKSTN-MBR-B**, log on using the **adatum\Administrator** account and the **Pa$$w0rd** password.

2. Click the **Desktop** tile. The *Desktop* appears.

3. Click the **File Explorer** button on the Taskbar. The *File Explorer* window appears.

4. In *File Explorer*, create a new folder on the *C:* drive named **C:\Users\Documents**.

5. Browse to the **C:\Windows\Logs** folder and copy its contents to the **C:\Users\Documents** folder you created.

6. Right-click the **Documents** folder you created and, from the context menu, choose **Properties**. The *Documents Properties* sheet appears.

7. Click the **Sharing** tab and then click **Advanced Sharing**. The *Advanced Sharing* dialog box appears.

8. Select the *Share this folder* check box and then click **Permissions**. The *Permissions for Documents* dialog box appears.

9. Ensure that *Everyone* is highlighted, select the **Allow Full Control** check box, and then click **OK**.

10. Click **OK** to close the *Advanced Sharing* dialog box.

11. On the *Documents Properties* sheet, click the **Security** tab and then click **Edit**. The *Permissions for Documents* dialog box appears (see Figure 15-1).

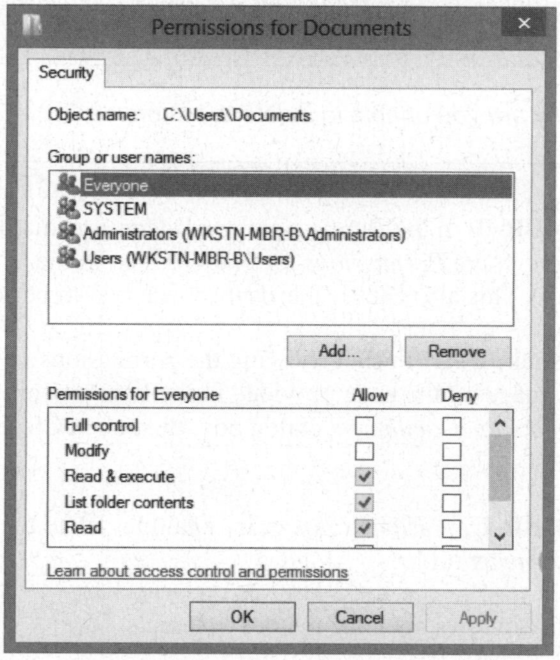

Figure 15-1
The *Permissions for Documents* dialog box

12. Click **Add**. The *Select Users, Computers, Service Accounts, or Groups* dialog box appears.

13. In the *Enter the object names to select* box, type **Student** and then click **OK**. The Student user appears in the *Group or user names* list in the *Permissions for support* dialog box.

14. Click **Apply**.

Question 1	*What permissions are assigned to the Student user by default?*

15. On **WKSTN-MBR-C**, log on using the **adatum\Student** account and the **Pa$$w0rd** password. Wait for the Student profile to complete.

16. Click the **Desktop** tile. The *Desktop* appears.

17. Click the **File Explorer** button on the Taskbar. The *File Explorer* window appears.

18. Expand the **Network** container and browse to the *\\WKSTN-MBR-B\Users\Documents* folder.

19. Right-click the SettingSync subfolder in the *Documents* folder and choose **Delete**. Click Yes to delete. Click Cancel to close the Folder Access Denied message.

Question 2	*Why are you unable to delete the subfolder?*

20. Back on **WKSTN-MBR-B**, in the *Permissions for Documents* dialog box, select the **Student** user and then, in the *Permissions for Student* box, in the *Allow* column, select the **Modify** check box. This also causes the *Write* check box to be selected.

21. Press **Alt+Prt Scr** to take a screen shot showing the permissions you added. Press **Ctrl+V** to paste the image on the page provided in the Lab 15 worksheet file. Click **OK** to close the *Permissions for Documents* dialog box, then click Close to close the Documents Properties.

22. Back on **WKSTN-MBR-C**, in *File Explorer*, try again to delete the SettingSync subfolder in the *Documents* folder.

End of exercise. Leave all windows open for the next exercise.

Exercise 15.2	Configuring NTFS Quotas
Overview	In this exercise, you will configure a disk to limit a user's storage space to 1 MB.
Mindset	NTFS quotas enable you to regulate the amount of disk space utilized by individual users.
Completion time	10 minutes

1. On the **WKSTN-MBR-B** workstation, in *File Explorer,* right-click the **Local Disk (C:)** container and choose **Properties**. The *Local Disk (C:) Properties* sheet appears.
2. Click the **Quota** tab (see Figure 15-2).

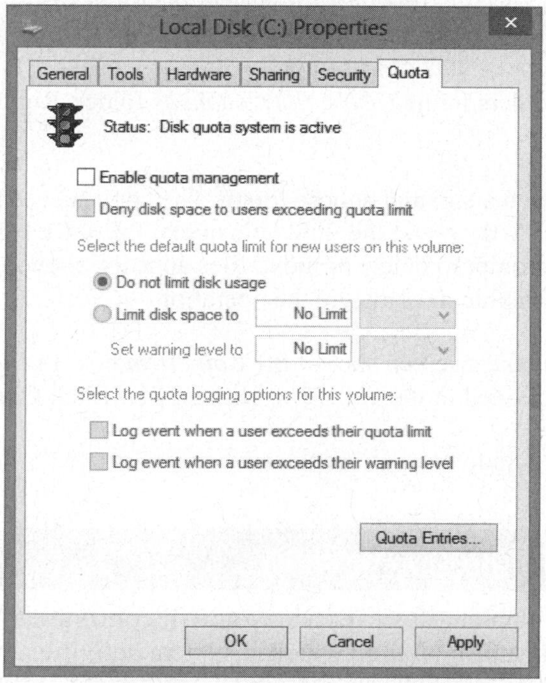

Figure 15-2
The *Quota* tab of a disk's Properties sheet

Question 3	*Why does the Quota tab only appear in the Properties sheet for volumes?*

3. Select the **Enable quota management** check box and the **Deny disk space to users exceeding quota limit** check box.

4. Click **Quota Entries**. The *Quota Entries for C:* dialog box appears.

5. From the *Quota* menu, click **New Quota Entry**. The *Select Users* dialog box appears.

6. In the *Enter the object names to select* text box, type **Student** and then click **OK**. The *Add New Quota Entry* dialog box appears.

7. Select the **Limit disk space to** option, specify **1 MB** for the limit, and then click **OK**. The Student user appears in the *Quota Entries* list. Observe that the percent used is 0. The folders currently in the Documents folder were copied there by the Domain Administrator and will not count against the Student quota. Close the Quota Entries window, click OK to close Local Disk (C:) Properties, then click OK to enable the quota system now.

8. On **WKSTN-MBR-C**, in *File Explorer*, browse to the same WKSTN-MBR-B share, **C:\Users\Documents,** that you accessed in Exercise 15.1.

9. Select all of the subfolders in the *C:\Users\Documents* folder. Right-click the selection and choose **Copy**.

10. Right-click the selection again and choose **Paste**. The copy succeeded because the added folders are less than 1 MB, within the Student's quota. Press **Ctrl+V** to copy the folders again. A Copy Item prompt to delete or move files appears, showing that there is not enough disk space available to complete the operation.

11. Press **Alt+Prt Scr** to take a screen shot of the *Copy Item* box. Press **Ctrl+V** to paste the image on the page provided in the Lab 15 worksheet file. Click **Cancel** to close the box.

End of exercise. Leave all windows open for the next exercise.

Exercise 15.3	Configuring Auditing
Overview	To complete this exercise, you will configure a Windows 8 workstation to audit specific system activities.
Mindset	In an enterprise environment, administrators typically use Active Directory-based Group Policy to configure auditing.
Completion time	20 minutes

1. On **WKSTN-MBR-B**, mouse over the lower-right corner of the window and, when the Charms bar appears, click **Search**.

2. Type **Administrative Tools** and then click **Settings**. Then click the **Administrative Tools** tile. The *Administrative Tools* window appears.

3. Double-click **Local Security Policy**. The *Local Security Policy* window appears.

4. Browse to the **Security Settings\Local Policies\Audit Policy** folder. The audit policies appear in the right pane.

5. Double-click the **Audit account logon events** policy. The *Audit account logon events Properties* sheet appears.

6. Select the **Failure** check box, clear the **Success** check box, and then click **OK**.

Question 4	*Why, in this case, is the auditing of event failures more useful than the auditing of successes?*

7. Double-click the **Audit object access** policy. The *Audit object access Properties* sheet appears.

8. Select the **Failure** check box, select the **Success** check box, and then click **OK**.

9. Press **Alt+Prt Scr** to take a screen shot showing the policies you configured. Press **Ctrl+V** to paste the image on the page provided in the Lab 15 worksheet file.

10. In *File Explorer*, browse to the **C:** drive on the local computer.

11. Right-click the **C:\Windows** folder and choose **Properties**. The *Windows Properties* sheet appears.

12. Click the **Security** tab and then click **Advanced**. The *Advanced Security Settings for Windows* dialog box appears.

13. Click the **Auditing** tab (see Figure 15-3).

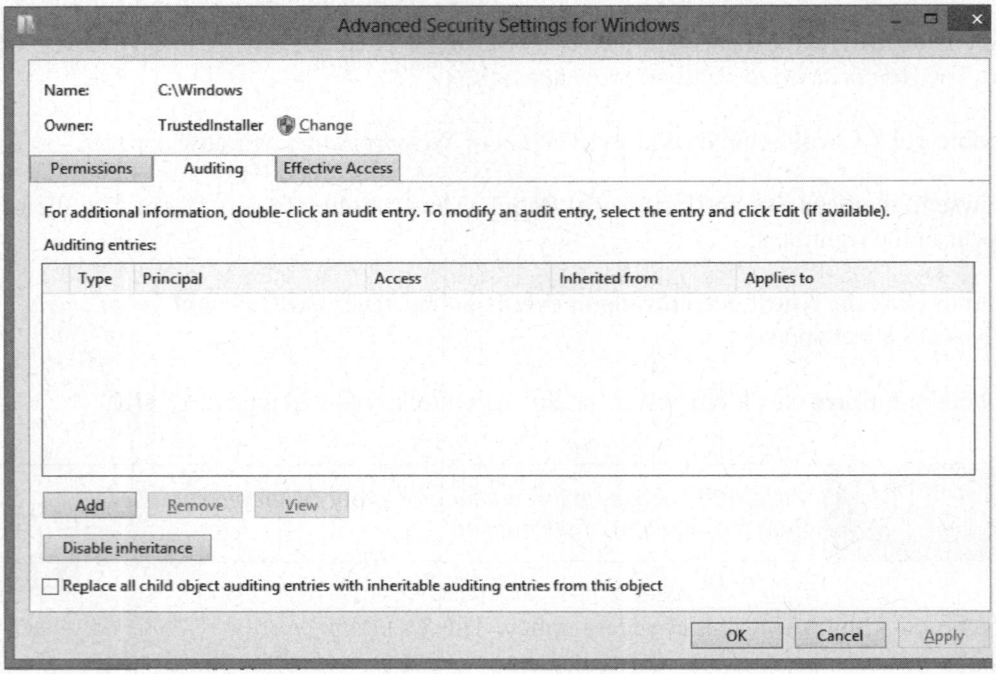

Figure 15-3
The *Advanced Security Settings for Windows* dialog box

14. Click **Add**. The *Auditing Entry for Windows* dialog box appears.

15. Click **Select a Principal**. The *Select User, Computer, Service Account, or Group* dialog box appears.

16. In the *Enter the object name to select* text box, type **Administrator** and then click **OK**.

17. Select the **Full Control** check box and then click **OK**.

18. Click **OK** to close the *Advanced Security Settings for Windows* dialog box, bypassing any error messages that appear.

19. Click **OK** to close the *Windows Properties* sheet.

20. Open an administrative Command Prompt window and type **gpupdate/force** to update the system's Group Policy settings.

End of exercise. Close all windows except Administrative Tools.

Lab Challenge	Viewing Auditing Data
Overview	To complete this exercise, you must demonstrate that your SVR-MBR-B computer is actually gathering the auditing data you configured its policies to gather.
Mindset	How do you display auditing data?
Completion time	10 minutes

To complete this challenge, display the auditing data you configured your server to gather in Exercise 15.3. Press **Alt+Prt Scr** to take a screen shot showing a sample of the data you gathered. Press **Ctrl+V** to paste the image on the page provided in the Lab 15 worksheet file.

End of lab.

LAB 16
CONFIGURING LOCAL SECURITY SETTINGS

THIS LAB CONTAINS THE FOLLOWING EXERCISES AND ACTIVITIES:

Exercise 16.1 Configuring Security Policy

Exercise 16.2 Configuring User Account Control Behavior

Exercise 16.3 Configuring Smart Screen Filter

Lab Challenge Configuring Secure Boot

BEFORE YOU BEGIN

The lab environment consists of computers connected to a local area network. The computers required for this lab are listed in Table 16-1.

Table 16-1
Computers Required for Lab 16

Computer	*Operating System*	*Computer Name*
Server	Windows Server 2012	SVR-DC-A
Client	Windows 7 Enterprise	WKSTN-MBR-C

In addition to the computers, you will also need the software listed in Table 16-2 to complete Lab 16.

Table 16-2
Software Required for Lab 16

Software	***Location***
Lab 16 student worksheet	Lab16_worksheet.docx (provided by instructor)

Working with Lab Worksheets

Each lab in this manual requires that you answer questions, shoot screen shots, and perform other activities that you will document in a worksheet named for the lab, such as Lab16_worksheet.docx. You will find these worksheets on the book companion site. It is recommended that you use a USB flash drive to store your worksheets, so you can submit them to your instructor for review. As you perform the exercises in each lab, open the appropriate worksheet file, type the required information, and then save the file to your flash drive.

SCENARIO

After completing this lab, you will be able to:

- Configure the local security policy including account and password policy
- Configure UAC
- Enable and disable SmartScreen Filter

Estimated lab time: 80 minutes

Exercise 16.1	Configuring Security Policy
Overview	In this exercise, you will modify the Default Domain Policy to set the account and password policy.
Mindset	To help ensure that users are using secure passwords, that passwords are changed regularly, and that a hacker does not keep trying different passwords, you can configure the account and password policy.
Completion time	40 minutes

1. On **SVR-DC-A**, log in using the **adatum\administrator** account and the **Pa$$w0rd** password.
2. When *Server Manager* opens, click **Tools > Active Directory Users and Computers**.
3. Right-click **Users OU**, click **New**, and then click **User**.

4. When the *New Object – User* dialog box opens (see Figure 16-1), type the following information, and then click **Next**.

   First name: **Tiffany**

   Last Name: **Columb**

   User logon name: **TiffanyC**

5. On the *Password* page (see Figure 16-1), type the following information and then click **Next**.

   Password: **P@ssword1**

   Confirm password: **P@ssword1**

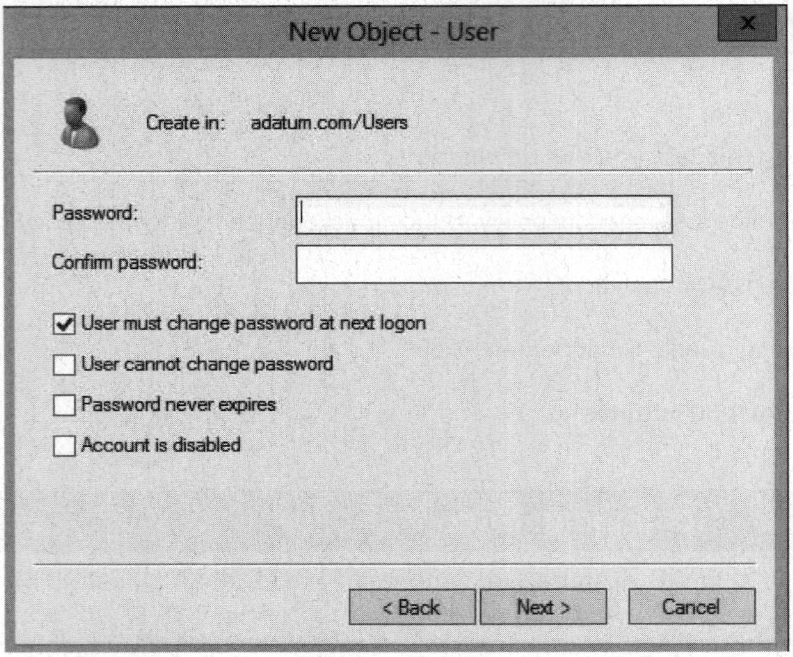

Figure 16-1
Configuring password settings

6. Click to deselect **User must change password at next logon**.

7. Click to select **Password never expires**. Click **Next**.

8. Click **Finish**.

9. When Server Manager appears, click **Tools > Group Policy Management**.

10. Navigate to **Forest:adatum.com>Domains>adatum.com**, expand the **adatum.com** domain, and then right-click **Default Domain Policy** and choose **Edit**.

11. When the *Group Policy Management Editor* opens, expand **Computer Configuration**, expand **Policies**, expand **Windows Settings**, expand **Security Settings**, expand **Account Policies**, and then click **Password Policy**.

Question 1	*What is the Minimum Password length?*

Question 2	*What is the maximum password age?*

12. Click the **Account Lockout Policy** node.

Question 3	*What is the Account lockout threshold?*

13. In the right pane, double-click **Account lockout threshold**.

14. On the *Local Security Setting* tab, type **3** for the number of invalid logon attempts and then click **OK**.

15. When the *Suggested Value Changes* box appears, answer Questions 4 and 5, then click **OK**.

Question 4	*What is the Account lockout duration?* 30 minutes.

Question 5	*What is the reset account lockout counter after set to?* 30 minutes.

16. In the right pane, double-click **Account lockout duration** (see Figure 16-2).

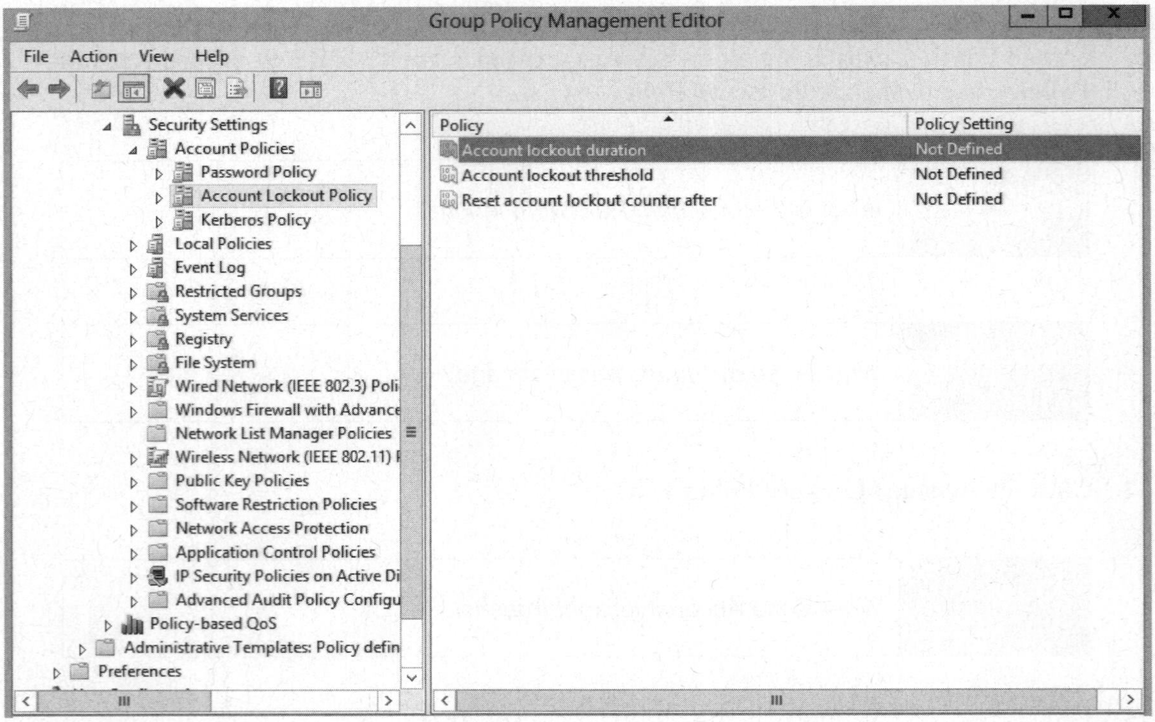

Figure 16-2
Setting the account lockout duration

17. On the *Security Policy Setting* tab, type **3** for the number of minutes and then click **OK**.

18. When the *Suggested Value Changes* box appears, click **OK**.

19. Take a screen shot of the *Policy and Policy Setting* pane by pressing **Alt+Prt Scr** and then paste it into your Lab 16 worksheet file in the page provided by pressing **Ctrl+V**.

20. To simulate a lockout, you are going to login with the TiffanyC account with the wrong password by logging in to **WKSTN-MBR-C** as **adatum\TiffanyC** with the **Password** password. Attempt this same password three more times.

Question 6	*What error message did you get?*

21. Click **OK**.

22. Go back to **SVR-DC-A**. Using **Active Directory Users and Computers**, double-click the **Tiffany Columb** account.

23. When the *Properties* dialog box opens, click the **Account** tab.

24. Click to select **Unlock account** and then click **OK**.

25. Go back to WKSTN-MBR-C and log in as **adatum\TiffanyC** with the **Password** password. Log in three more times until the account is locked again.

26. Wait three minutes. Then log in as **adatum\TiffanyC** with the **Pa$$w0rd** password.
Adatum\Administrator 2

27. In the upper-right corner, click the currently logged-on user and then click **Sign out**.

28. Go back to **SVR-DC-A** and go back to the **Group Policy Management Editor**.

29. Double-click the **Account lockout threshold** option.

30. When the *Account lockout threshold Properties* dialog box opens, change the value to **0** and then click **OK**.

31. When the *Suggested Value Changes* dialog box opens, click **OK**.

32. Close the **Group Policy Management Editor** and then close **Group Policy Management**.

33. Close **Active Directory Users and Computers**.

End of exercise. Leave the SVR-DC-A logged in for the next exercise.

Exercise 16.2	Configuring User Account Control Behavior
Overview	In this exercise, you will configure the UAC on a workstation, and then modify the local security policy to control the UAC settings.
Mindset	The User Account Control helps protect the system by preventing programs from performing unauthorized actions, However, sometimes you will need to modify the User Account Control settings so that your programs will run properly.
Completion time	20 minutes

1. Log in to **WKSTN-MBR-C** as **adatum\TiffanyC**.

2. Click the **Desktop** tile.

3. Mouse over the lower-left corner of the desktop and right-click the **Start** screen thumbnail that appears there. Then click **Control Panel**.

4. Using the *Control Panel*, in the *Search Control Panel* text box, type **UAC**

5. Under *Action Center*, click **Change user Account Control settings**.

6. Notice that the screen dims. In the *User Account Control* dialog box, type the following:

   User name: **adatum\administrator**

Password: **Pa$$w0rd**

Click Yes.

Question 7	*On the User Account Control Settings page, what was the default UAC setting?*

7. On the *User Account Control Settings* page (see Figure 16-3), click and drag the slider down to the **Always notify me (and do not dim my desktop) when:** setting, and then click **OK**.

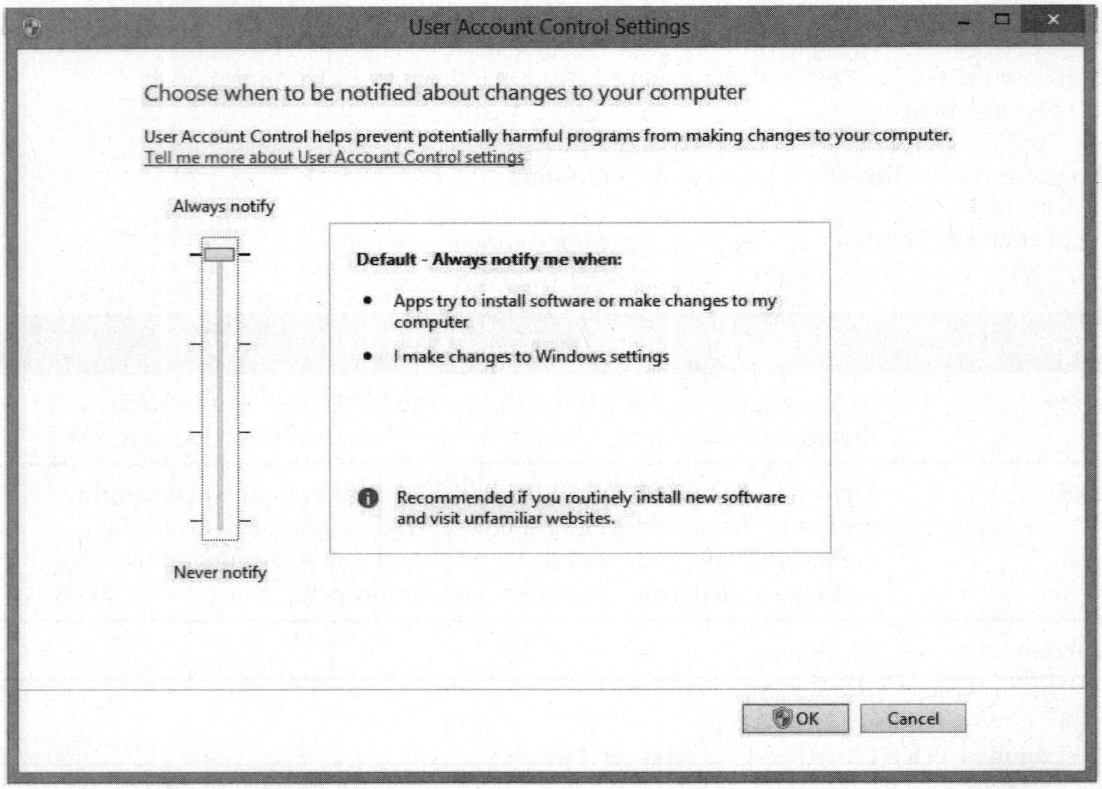

Figure 16-3
The *User Account Control Settings* page

8. In the *User Account Control* dialog box, type the following:

   User name: **adatum\administrator**

   Password: **Pa$$w0rd**

9. In the *UAC - Control Panel*, click the **Change User Account Control settings** option again. Notice that the screen does not dim this time.

10. At the *User Account Control* dialog box, type the following and then click **Yes**:

    User name: **adatum\administrator**

    Password: **Pa$$w0rd**

11. Slide the slider back to **Default - Always notify me when:,** and then click **OK**.

12. In the *User Account Control* dialog box, type the following and then click **Yes**:

    User name: **adatum\administrator**

    Password: **Pa$$w0rd**

13. Log off as **adatum\TiffanyC**.

14. Log on as **adatum\administrator** with the **Pa$$w0rd** password.

15. In the *Start* screen, type **secpol.msc** and press **Enter**.

16. When the *Local Security Policy* console opens, expand **Local Policies** and then click **Security Options**.

17. Scroll down to the bottom of the policy list until you see the 10 policies with the User Account Control prefix.

18. Double-click the **User Account Control: Behavior of the elevation prompt for standard users** policy.

19. On the *Local Security Setting* tab, click the drop-down arrow, choose **Automatically deny elevation requests**, and then click **OK**.

20. Take a screen shot of the *Local Security Policy* console by pressing **Alt+Prt Scr** and then paste it into your Lab 16 worksheet file in the page provided by pressing **Ctrl+V**.

21. Close the **Local Security Policy**.

22. Log off as **adatum\administrator**.

23. Log on as **adatum\TiffanyC** with the **Pa$$w0rd** password.

24. On the *Start* screen, type **diskmgmt.msc** and then press **Enter**.

Question 8	*What error message is displayed?*

25. Click **OK** to close the *Disk Management* dialog box.

26. Close **Disk Management**.

27. Log off as TiffanyC.

End of exercise. Leave the computers running for the next exercise.

Exercise 16.3	Configuring SmartScreen Filter
Overview	In this exercise, you will enable and then disable the SmartScreen filter in Internet Explorer.
Mindset	To help maintain the security on organization's computers, SmartScreen Filters is designed to keep your computer safe by warning you before you run apps or files from the Internet that are considered to be unsafe.
Completion time	10 minutes

1. Log in to **WKSTN-MBR-C** as **adatum\administrator** with the **Pa$$w0rd** password.

2. From the *Windows 8 Start* screen, click the **Desktop** tile.

3. On the task bar, click the **Internet Explorer** icon.

4. Press **Alt+X** and then click **Safety > Turn off SmartScreen Filter**.

5. In the *Microsoft SmartScreen Filter* window (see Figure 16-4), confirm *Turn off SmartScreen Filter* is selected and then click **OK**.

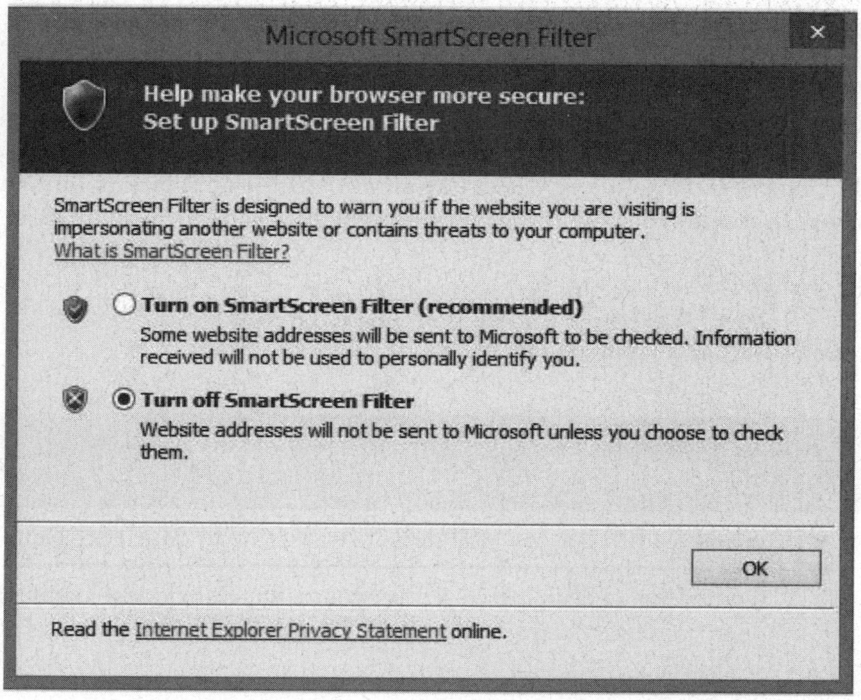

Figure 16-4
The *Microsoft SmartScreen Filter* dialog box

6. Press the **Alt+X**, click **Safety > Turn on SmartScreen Filter**, and then click **OK**.

7. Close the *Internet Explorer* browser window.

8. Mouse over the lower-left corner of the desktop and click the **Start** screen thumbnail that appears there to open the *Start Menu*.

9. Type **Control Panel** and then press **Enter**.

10. When the *Control Panel* opens, in the *Search Control Panel* text box, type **Change SmartScreen settings**.

Question 9	*Where is the Change SmartScreen settings found in the Control Panel?*

11. Click **Change SmartScreen settings**.

12. In the *Windows SmartScreen* box, select **Don't do anything (turn off Windows SmartScreen)** and then click **OK**.

13. After making this change, a warning message displays under the *Security* section, recommending that you keep Windows SmartScreen enabled.

14. Take a screen shot of the *Action Center* by pressing **Alt+Prt Scr** and then paste it into your Lab 16 worksheet file in the page provided by pressing **Ctrl+V**.

15. In the left pane of the *Action Center*, click **Change Windows SmartScreen settings**.

16. In the *Windows SmartScreen* box, select **Get administrator approval before running an unrecognized app from the Internet (recommended)** and then click **OK**.

17. Close the *Action Center* window.

End of exercise. Leave the computers running for the next exercise.

Lab Challenge	Configuring Secure Boot
Overview	In this challenge, you will demonstrate how to configure Secure Boot.
Mindset	Secure Boot is designed to protect your computer against loading malware when booting systems that have the Unified Extensible Firmware Interface (UEFI).
Completion time	10 minutes

To protect the boot process from malware, you can use SecureBoot. Therefore, during this lab challenge, you will write out the steps used to enable Secure Boot Mode. Since SecureBoot requires UEFI, this is only a written exercise.

End of lab.

LAB 17
CONFIGURING AUTHENTICATION AND AUTHORIZATION

THIS LAB CONTAINS THE FOLLOWING EXERCISES AND ACTIVITIES:

Exercise 17.1	Creating Local Users
Exercise 17.2	Managing Credentials
Lab Challenge	Assigning User Rights

BEFORE YOU BEGIN

The lab environment consists of computers connected to a local area network in a workgroup configuration. The computers required for this lab are listed in Table 17-1.

Table 17-1
Computers Required for Lab 17

Computer	*Operating System*	*Computer Name*
Server	Windows Server 2012	SVR-WKGRP-A
Workstation	Windows 8 Enterprise	WKSTN-WKGRP-B
Workstation	Windows 8 Enterprise	WKSTN-WKGRP-C

In addition to the computers, you will also need the software listed in Table 17-2 to complete Lab 17.

Table 17-2
Software Required for Lab 17

Software	*Location*
Lab 17 student worksheet	Lab17_worksheet.docx (provided by instructor)

Working with Lab Worksheets

Each lab in this manual requires that you answer questions, create screenshots, and perform other activities that you will document in a worksheet named for the lab, such as Lab17_worksheet.docx. You will find these worksheets on the book companion site. It is recommended that you use a USB flash drive to store your worksheets so you can submit them to your instructor for review. As you perform the exercises in each lab, open the appropriate worksheet file, type the required information, and then save the file to your flash drive.

SCENARIO

After completing this lab, you will be able to:

- Create local users and groups
- Configure user rights
- Manage credentials

Estimated lab time: 50 minutes

Exercise 17.1	Creating Local Users
Overview	In this exercise, you will create new local user accounts with the controls provided in the Windows 8 PC Settings screen.
Mindset	In a workgroup environment, users must have separate accounts on every computer they access.
Completion time	15 minutes

1. On WKSTN-MBR-B, log on using the **wkstn-wrkgrp-b\ocox** account and the **Pa$$w0rd** password.

2. Mouse over the lower right corner of the **Start** screen and, when the Charms bar appears, click **Settings > Change PC Settings**. The *PC Settings* screen appears.

3. Click **Users**. The *Users* page appears (see Figure 17-1).

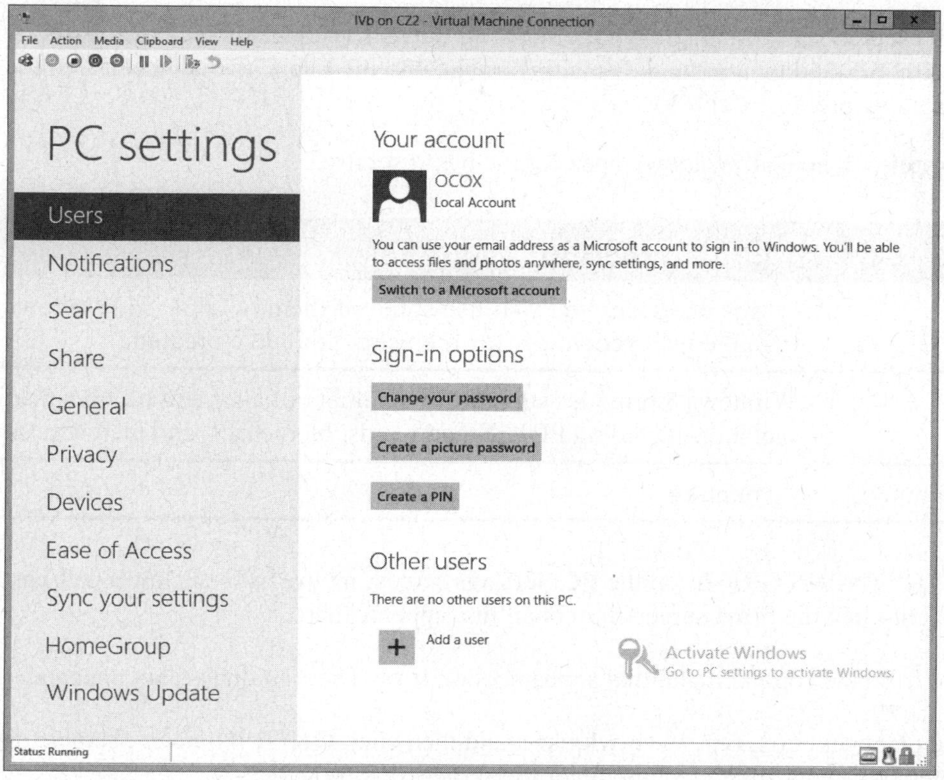

Figure 17-1
The *Users* page of the PC Settings *screen*

4. Click **Add a user**. The *Add a user* screen appears.

5. In the *User name* text box, type **JKotas**.

6. In the *Password* text box and the *Reenter password* text box, type **Pa$$w0rd**.

7. In the *Password hint* text box, type **hint** and then click **Next**. The system creates the user account.

8. Click **Finish**. The new account is added to the *Users* page.

Question 1	*What happens in Windows 8 when you try to create a user through the traditional method, using the User Control Panel?*

9. Repeat steps 4 to 8 to create two more users with the names **TAllen** and **AKol**, using the same password and password hint values shared in Step 6 and Step 7.

10. Take a screen shot of the *Users* page showing the new accounts you created by pressing **Ctrl+Prt Scr** and then paste the resulting image into the Lab 17 worksheet file in the page provided by pressing **Ctrl+V**.

End of exercise. Leave all windows open for the next exercise.

Exercise 17.2	Managing Credentials
Overview	In this exercise, you will use some of the new tools in Windows 8 to manage the credentials for the users you have created.
Mindset	Windows 8 provides support for a number of alternative authentication methods, including PINs, Smart Cards, biometrics, and picture passwords.
Completion time	20 minutes

1. On **WKSTN-WKGRP-B**, on the **PC Settings** screen, mouse over the lower-left corner and right-click the **Start** screen thumbnail that appears there.

2. Then, from the context menu that appears, click **Run**. The *Run* dialog box appears.

3. In the *Open* text box, type **\\svr-wkgrp-a** and then click **OK**. A *Windows Security* dialog box appears, requesting credentials for the server SVR-WKGRP-A.

4. Click **Cancel**.

Question 2	*Why are you unable to connect to SVR-WKGRP-A without supplying credentials?*

5. Mouse over the lower-left corner of the desktop and right-click the **Start** screen thumbnail that appears there. Then, from the context menu that appears, click **Control Panel**. The *Control Panel* appears.

6. Click **User Accounts and Family Safety > Credential Manager**. The *Credential Manager* control panel applet appears, as shown in Figure 17-2.

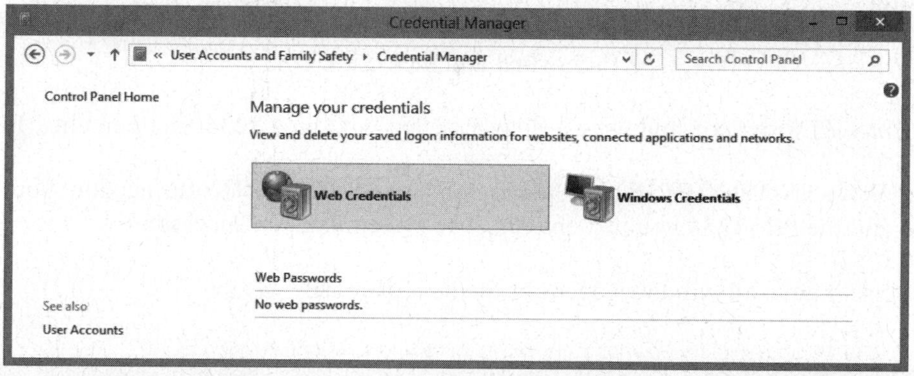

Figure 17-2
The *Credential Manager* control panel

7. Click **Windows Credentials** and then click **Add a Windows credential**. The *Add a Windows Credential* dialog box appears.

8. In the *Internet or network address* text box, type **SVR-WKGRP-A**.

9. In the *User name* text box, type **Administrator**.

10. In the *Password* text box, type **Pa$$w0rd** and then click **OK**. The credential appears in the *Windows Credentials* list.

11. Take a screen shot of the *Windows Credentials* control panel showing the new credential you entered by pressing **Ctrl+Prt Scr** and then paste the resulting image into the Lab 17 worksheet file in the page provided by pressing **Ctrl+V**.

12. Close the Credential Manager window, then open the **Run** dialog box again and try to connect to the **SVR-WKGRP-A** server. This time, the *File Explorer* window appears, displaying the shares on the remote computer.

Question 3	*Why are you now able to connect to SVR-WKGRP-A without supplying credentials?*

13. Log off **WKSTN-WKGRP-B** and log on again using the **JKotas** account you created and the **Pa$$w0rd** password.

14. Mouse over the lower right corner of the **Start** screen and, when the Charm bar appears, click **Settings > Change PC Settings**. The *PC Settings* screen appears.

15. Click **Users**. The *Users* page appears.

16. Click **Create a PIN**. A *Create a PIN* screen appears, prompting you to confirm your password.

17. In the *Password* text box, type **Pa$$w0rd** and then click **OK**.

18. In the *Enter PIN* text box and the *Confirm PIN* text box, type **1234** and then click **Finish**.

19. Log off **WKSTN-WKGRP-B** and then log on again using the **JKotas** account you created and the PIN **1234** you just entered. The system logs on successfully.

End of exercise. Leave all windows open for the next exercise.

Lab Challenge	Assigning User Rights
Overview	In this challenge, you will add a selection of user rights assignments to the ones that already exist.
Mindset	User rights provide specific users or groups with the ability to perform specific tasks on a computer running Windows 8.
Completion time	15 minutes

Your organization has created a new job role called the director, and your job is to provide the new directors with the user rights they need to perform their jobs. To complete this challenge, you must create the Directors group and add the three user accounts you created in Exercise 17.1 to that group. Then you must grant the Directors group the following user rights to your local system, without interfering with any of the existing rights:

- Deny logon locally
- Enable computer and user accounts to be trusted for delegation
- Force shutdown from a remote system
- Manage auditing and security log
- Shut down the system

Write out the basic steps you had to perform to accomplish the challenge and then shoot a screen shot showing the user rights you configured. Then press **Ctrl+V** to paste the image on the page provided in the Lab 17 worksheet file.

End of lab.

LAB 18
CONFIGURING REMOTE CONNECTIONS

THIS LAB CONTAINS THE FOLLOWING EXERCISES AND ACTIVITIES:

Exercise 18.1	Configuring a VPN Connection
Exercise 18.2	Connecting to a VPN Server
Lab Challenge	Testing VPN Protocols

BEFORE YOU BEGIN

The lab environment consists of computers connected to a local area network in an Active Directory Domain Services configuration. The computers required for this lab are listed in Table 18-1.

Table 18-1
Computers Required for Lab 18

Computer	***Operating System***	***Computer Name***
Server	Windows Server 2012	SVR-DC-A
Workstation	Windows 8 Enterprise	WKSTN-MBR-B

In addition to the computers, you will also need the software listed in Table 18-2 to complete Lab 18.

Table 18-2
Software Required for Lab 18

Software	***Location***
Lab 18 student worksheet	Lab18_worksheet.docx (provided by instructor)

Working with Lab Worksheets

Each lab in this manual requires that you answer questions, create screenshots, and perform other activities that you will document in a worksheet named for the lab, such as Lab18_worksheet.docx. You will find these worksheets on the book companion site. It is recommended that you use a USB flash drive to store your worksheets so you can submit them to your instructor for review. As you perform the exercises in each lab, open the appropriate worksheet file, type the required information, and then save the file to your flash drive.

SCENARIO

After completing this lab, you will be able to:

- Configure a VPN connection
- Establish a VPN connection

Estimated lab time: 40 minutes

Exercise 18.1	Configuring a VPN Connection
Overview	In this exercise, you will create a connection that enables the workstation to connect to your server using virtual private networking.
Mindset	VPNs use tunneling to create secure connections across a public network.
Completion time	20 minutes

1. On **WKSTN-MBR-B**, log on using the **adatum\Administrator** account and the **Pa$$w0rd** password.

2. Click the **Desktop** tile. The *Desktop* appears.

3. Mouse over the lower-left corner of the desktop and right-click the **Start** screen thumbnail that appears there. Then, from the context menu that appears, click **Control Panel**. The *Control Panel* window appears.

4. Click **Network and Internet > Network and Sharing Center**. The *Network and Sharing Center* control panel appears (see Figure 18-1).

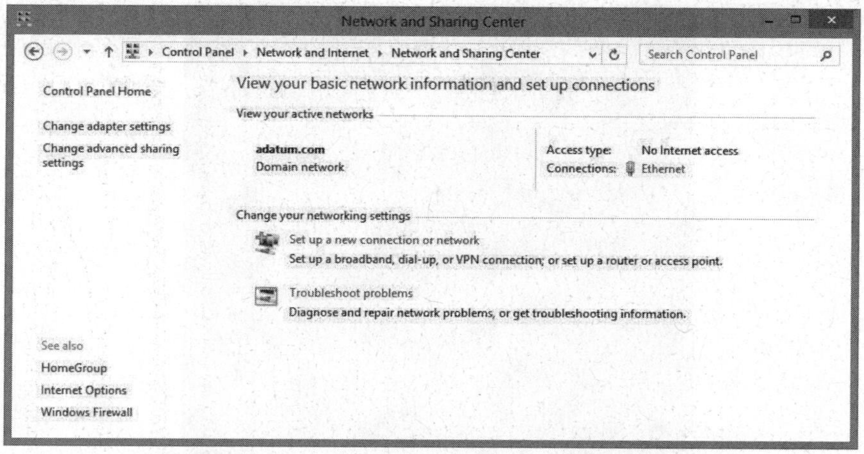

Figure 18-1
The *Network and Sharing Center* control panel

5. Click **Set up a new connection or network**. The *Set Up a Connection or Network Wizard* appears, displaying the *Choose a connection option* page.

6. Select **Connect to a workplace** and then click **Next**. The *How do you want to connect?* page appears.

7. Click **Use my Internet connection (VPN)**. The *Do you want to set up an Internet connection before continuing?* page appears.

> **NOTE**
> *For the purposes of this lab, the network does need not be connected to the Internet.*

8. Click **I'll set up an Internet connection later**. The *Type the Internet address to connect to* page appears.

9. In the *Internet address* text box, type **SVR-DC-A.adatum.com**.

10. In the *Destination name* text box, type **VPN Server Connection**.

11. Select the **Allow other people to use this connection** check box.

12. Take a screen shot of the *Connect to a Workplace* Wizard showing the page you just configured by pressing **Alt+Prt Scr**, and then paste the resulting image into the Lab 18 worksheet file in the page provided by pressing **Ctrl+V**.

13. Click **Create**. The wizard creates the connection and adds it to the *Connections* list on the fly-out menu (see Figure 18-2).

Figure 18-2
The *Connections* list in the Windows 8 fly-out menu

Question 1	*How many connections are there in the Network Connections window?*

14. On the fly-out menu, right-click **VPN Server Connection** and choose **View connection properties**. The *VPN Server Connection Properties* sheet appears.

15. Click the **Security** tab and then take a screen shot of the *VPN Server Connection Properties* sheet by pressing **Alt+Prt Scr**. Then paste the resulting image into the Lab 18 worksheet file in the page provided by pressing **Ctrl+V**.

16. Click the **Options** tab.

17. From the *Idle time before hanging up* drop-down list, select **5 minutes**.

18. Click **OK** to close the *VPN Server Connection Properties* sheet.

End of exercise. Leave all windows open for the next exercise.

Exercise 18.2	Connecting to a VPN Server
Overview	In this exercise, you will use the connection you created earlier to connect to your SVR-DC-A server using virtual private networking.
Mindset	During the connection establishment process, the two computers involved in a VPN connection authenticate each other and select a VPN protocol.
Completion time	10 minutes

1. On the Windows 8 desktop, click the network icon in the notification area (located at the lower-right corner of the screen). The *Networks* flyout menu appears.

2. Click **VPN Server Connection** and then click **Connect**. A *Network Authentication* tile appears (see Figure 18-3).

Figure 18-3
The *Network Authentication* dialog box

3. In the *User name* text box, type **Administrator**. In the *Password* text box, type **Pa$$w0rd**. Then click **OK**. The workstation connects to the VPN server and the connection appears in the *Networks* list with a *Connected* indicator.

4. Right-click the **VPN Server Connection** link and click the View network status option. The *VPN Server Connection Status* dialog box appears.

5. Click the **Details** tab (not the Details button).

Question 2	*Which VPN protocol is the connection using?*

Question 3	*Which authentication protocol is the VPN connection using?*

6. Take a screen shot of the *VPN Server Connection Status* dialog box by pressing **Alt+Prt Scr** and then paste the resulting image into the Lab 18 worksheet file in the page provided by pressing **Ctrl+V**.

End of exercise. Close any open windows before you begin the next exercise.

Lab Challenge	Testing VPN Protocols
Overview	By default, the Windows 8 VPN client is configured to select a VPN type automatically. In this challenge, you configure the client to use each of its supported VPN types to then determine which ones are currently supported by your VPN server.
Mindset	Windows VPN clients and servers each supports a variety of connection protocols with different authentication requirements and levels of security.
Completion time	10 minutes

To complete this challenge, open the Properties sheet for the VPN connection you created in Exercise 18.1, click the Security tab, and then select each of the four specific Type of VPN values in turn, attempting to connect to the server with each one. Record your results in Table 18-3 on your worksheet.

Table 18-3
Connection Results for VPN Protocols

Type of VPN	*Result message*
Point-to-Point Tunneling Protocol	
Layer 2 Tunneling Protocol with IPsec (L2TP/IPSec)	
Secure Socket Tunneling Protocol (SSTP)	
IKEv2	

End of lab.

LAB 19
CONFIGURING MOBILITY OPTIONS

THIS LAB CONTAINS THE FOLLOWING EXERCISES AND ACTIVITIES:

Exercise 19.1	Configuring Power Options
Exercise 19.2	Creating a Custom Power Plan
Lab Challenge	Using Powercfg.exe

BEFORE YOU BEGIN

The lab environment consists of computers connected to a local area network in an Active Directory Domain Services configuration. The computers required for this lab are listed in Table 19-1.

Table 19-1
Computers Required for Lab 19

Computer	*Operating System*	*Computer Name*
Server	Windows Server 2012	SVR-DC-A
Workstation	Windows 8 Enterprise	WKSTN-MBR-B
Workstation	Windows 8 Enterprise	WKSTN-MBR-C

In addition to the computers, you will also need the software listed in Table 19-2 to complete Lab 19.

Table 19-2
Software Required for Lab 19

Software	*Location*
Lab 19 student worksheet	Lab19_worksheet.docx (provided by instructor)

Working with Lab Worksheets

Each lab in this manual requires that you answer questions, create screenshots, and perform other activities that you will document in a worksheet named for the lab, such as Lab19_worksheet.docx. You will find these worksheets on the book companion site. It is recommended that you use a USB flash drive to store your worksheets so you can submit them to your instructor for review. As you perform the exercises in each lab, open the appropriate worksheet file, type the required information in Word, and then save the file to your flash drive.

SCENARIO

After completing this lab, you will be able to:

- Configure power options
- Create a custom power plan
- Use powercfg.exe

Estimated lab time: 50 minutes

Exercise 19.1	Configuring Power Options
Overview	In this exercise, you will examine the power settings used in the default power plans provided in Windows.
Mindset	Windows 8 provides a range of settings that you can use to conserve power.
Completion time	20 minutes

1. On **WKSTN-MBR-B**, log on using the **adatum\Administrator** account and the **Pa$$w0rd** password.
2. Click the **Desktop** tile. The *Desktop* appears.

3. Mouse over the lower-left corner of the desktop and right-click the **Start** screen thumbnail that appears there. Then, from the context menu that appears, click **Control Panel**. The *Control Panel* window appears.

4. Click **Hardware and Sound > Power Options**. The *Power Options* control panel appears (see Figure 19-1).

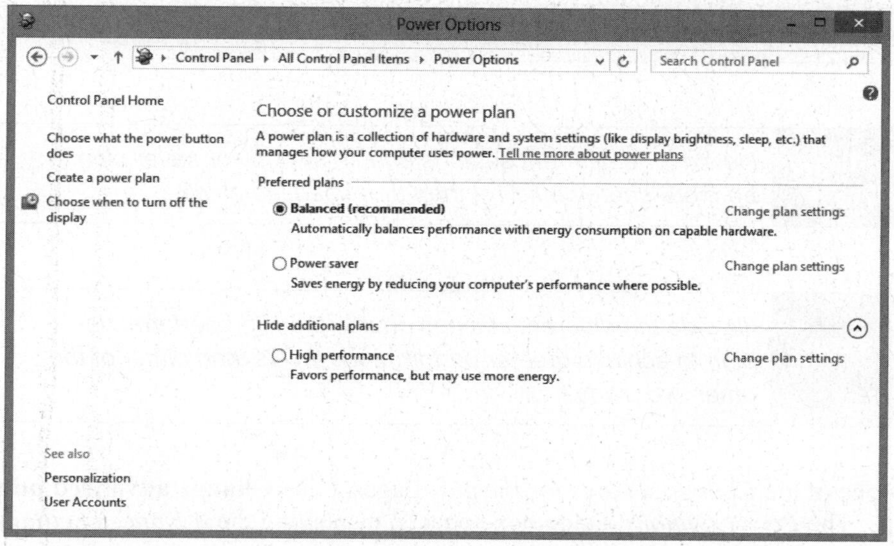

Figure 19-1
The *Power Options* control panel

5. Click the **Show additional plans** down-arrow.

Question 1	*How many power plans are available for your selection in the Power Options control panel?*

6. In the Balanced plan option, click the **Change plan settings** link. The *Change settings for the plan: Balanced* page appears.

7. In cell Table 19-3, enter the value for the *Turn off the display* setting.

8. Click **Cancel**.

9. Click the **Change plan settings** link for the *Power saver* plan and then enter the values for the *Turn off the display* setting into the appropriate cells of Table 19-3. Click Cancel.

10. Click the **Change plan settings** link for the *High performance* plan and then type the values for the *Turn off the display* setting into the appropriate cells of Table 19-3. Click Cancel.

Table 19-3
Default Windows 8 Power Configuration Settings

Setting	*Balanced*	*Power Saver*	*High Performance*
Turn off the display			

Question 2	*How do the different settings enable the Power saver plan to be more energy efficient than the Balanced plan?*

Question 3	*How do the different settings enable the High performance plan to achieve greater performance levels than either of the other two plans?*

11. In any one of the *Change settings for the plan* pages, click **Change advanced power settings**. The *Power Options* dialog box appears, displaying the *Advanced Settings* tab.

12. Take a screen shot of the *Power Options* dialog box by pressing **Alt+Prt Scr** and then paste the resulting image into the Lab 19 worksheet file in the page provided by pressing **Ctrl+V**.

13. Using the drop-down list to change power plans, examine the values for the advanced power settings and type them in Table 19-4.

Table 19-4
Default Windows 7 Advanced Power Configuration Settings

Setting	*Balanced*	*Power Saver*	*High Performance*
Turn off hard disk after			
Internet Explorer \ JavaScript Timer Frequency			
Desktop background settings \ Slide show			
Wireless Adapter Settings \ Power Saving Mode			
Sleep \ Allow wake timers			
USB settings \ USB selective suspend setting			

Power buttons and lid \ Power button action			
PCI Express \ Link State Power Management			
Processor power management \ System cooling policy			
Display \ Turn off display after			
Display \ Enable adaptive brightness			
Multimedia settings \ When sharing media			
Multimedia settings \ When playing video			

Question 4	*Which of the settings on the Advanced settings tab enables the Power saver plan to conserve more energy than the other two plans?*

14. Click **OK** to close the *Power Options* dialog box.

End of exercise. Leave all windows open for the next exercise.

Exercise 19.2	Creating a Custom Power Plan
Overview	In this exercise, you will create power plans for your company's desktop and laptop workstations.
Mindset	Desktop and portable computers have different power requirements and therefore require separate power plans.
Completion time	20 minutes

1. On **WKSTN-MBR-B**, in the *Power Options* control panel, click **Create a power plan**. The *Create a Power Plan* Wizard appears (see Figure 19-2).

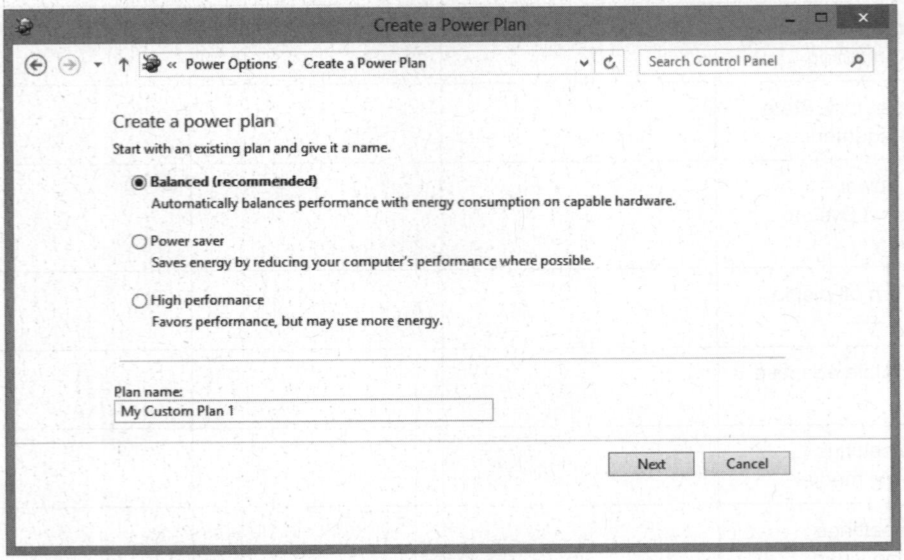

Figure 19-2
The *Create a Power Plan* Wizard

2. Leave the *Balanced (recommended)* option selected and, in the *Plan name* text box, type **Adatum Desktops** and then click **Next**. The *Change settings for the plan: Adatum Desktops* page appears.

3. In the *Turn off the display* drop-down list, select **15 minutes**.

4. Click **Create**. The *Adatum Desktops* plan appears in the *Power Options* control panel.

5. Repeat steps 2 thru 4 to create another power plan called **Adatum Laptops** with the *Turn off the display* setting set to **5 minutes**.

6. Take a screen shot of the *Power Options* control panel, showing the power plans you created, by pressing **Alt+Prt Scr** and then paste the resulting image into the Lab 19 worksheet file in the page provided by pressing **Ctrl+V**.

7. Click the **Change plan settings** link for the *Adatum Desktops* plan. The *Change settings for the plan: Adatum Desktops* page appears.

8. Click **Change advanced power settings**. The *Power Options* dialog box appears, displaying the *Advanced Settings* tab.

9. Make sure that *Adatum Desktops* is selected in the drop-down list and then configure the following settings:

- Turn off hard disk after: 15 minutes
- PCI Express \ Link State Power Management: Maximum power savings

- Processor power management \ System cooling policy: Active
- Multimedia settings \ When playing video: Optimize power savings

10. Click **OK** to close the *Power Options* dialog box.

11. Click **Cancel** to close the *Change settings for the plan: Adatum Desktops* page.

12. Open the *Change settings for the plan: Adatum Laptops* page and then click **Change advanced power settings**. The *Power Options* dialog box appears, displaying the *Advanced Settings* tab.

13. Make sure that *Adatum Laptops* is selected in the drop-down list and then configure the following settings:

    - Turn off hard disk after: 5 minutes
    - Wireless adapter settings \ Power saving mode: Maximum power saving
    - PCI Express \ Link State Power Management: Maximum power savings
    - Processor power management \ System cooling policy: Passive
    - Multimedia settings \ When playing video: Optimize power savings

14. Click **OK** to close the *Power Options* dialog box.

Question 5	*Why does the Adatum Laptops power plan have a setting to maximize wireless adapter power savings, which the Adatum Desktops plan does not?*

15. Close the *Power Options* control panel.

End of exercise. Leave all windows open for the next exercise.

Lab Challenge	Using Powercfg.exe
Overview	Now that you have created power plans for your company's desktop and laptop computers, you must determine how to transfer those plans to other computers.
Mindset	You can use the Powercfg.exe command-line utility to export your power plans from your WKSTN-MBR-B workstation and import them on WKSTN-MBR-C.
Completion time	10 minutes

In this challenge, you will use the Powercfg.exe command-line utility to export your power plans from your WKSTN-MBR-B workstation and import them on WKSTN-MBR-C.

To complete the challenge, you must perform the following tasks:

1. Use the Powercfg.exe utility to display the 32-character GUID values for the power plans you created in Exercise 19.2, and then copy the GUID values into Table 19-5.

Table 19-5
Custom Power Plan GUIDs

Power Plan Name	***32-character GUID***
Adatum Desktops	
Adatum Laptops	

2. Write the commands needed to export the power plans you created on WKSTN-MBR-B to files, copy the files to the Downloads share on SVR-DC-A, and then import the power plans on WKSTN-MBR-C.

3. Execute the commands on the two workstations and take screen shots of each by pressing **Alt+Prt Scr** and then paste the two resulting images into the Lab 19 worksheet file in the page provided by pressing **Ctrl+V**.

End of lab.

LAB 20
CONFIGURING SECURITY FOR MOBILE DEVICES

THIS LAB CONTAINS THE FOLLOWING EXERCISES AND ACTIVITIES:

Exercise 20.1	Configuring BitLocker
Exercise 20.2	Creating a Data Recovery Agent (DRA)
Exercise 20.3	Disabling the Windows Location Provider
Lab Challenge	Performing a Remote Wipe using the Exchange Admin Center (EAC)

BEFORE YOU BEGIN

The lab environment consists of student workstations connected to a local area network, along with a server that functions as the domain controller for a domain called adatum.com. The computers required for this lab are listed in Table 20-1.

Table 20-1
Computers Required for Lab 20

Computer	***Operating System***	***Computer Name***
Server (VM 1)	Windows Server 2012	SVR-DC-A
Client (VM 3)	Windows 7 Enterprise	WKSTN-MBR-C

In addition to the computers, you will also need the software listed in Table 20-2 to complete Lab 20.

Table 20-2
Software Required for Lab 20

Software	***Location***
Lab 20 student worksheet	Lab20_worksheet.docx (provided by instructor)

Working with Lab Worksheets

Each lab in this manual requires that you answer questions, shoot screen shots, and perform other activities that you will document in a worksheet named for the lab, such as Lab20_worksheet.docx. You will find these worksheets on the book companion site. It is recommended that you use a USB flash drive to store your worksheets so you can submit them to your instructor for review. As you perform the exercises in each lab, open the appropriate worksheet file, type the required information, and then save the file to your flash drive.

SCENARIO

After completing this lab, you will be able to:

- Enable and configure BitLocker
- Install the Certificate Authority
- Request a certificate from a Certificate Authority
- Disable the Windows Location Provider
- Create a Data Recovery Agent (DRA) for EFS
- Perform a Remote Wipe using the Exchange Admin Center (EAC)

Estimated lab time: 70 minutes

Exercise 20.1	Configuring BitLocker
Overview	In this exercise, you will enable BitLocker for the volume containing the operating system.
Completion time	20 minutes

1. On **WKSTN-MBR-C**, log on using the **adatum\administrator** account and the **Pa$$w0rd** password.

2. On the *Start* screen, type **gpedit.msc**, and then press **Enter**.

3. When the Local Group Policy Editor opens, navigate to **\Computer Configuration\Administrative Templates\Windows Components\BitLocker Drive Encryption\Operating System Drives** and then double-click **Require additional authentication at startup**.

4. When the *Require additional authentication at startup* dialog box opens, click **Enabled**.

5. Take a screen shot of the local policy setting by pressing **Alt+Prt Scr** and then paste it into your Lab 20 worksheet file in the page provided by pressing **Ctrl+V**.

6. Click **OK** to close the *Require additional authentication at startup* dialog box.

7. Close **Local Group Policy Editor**.

8. Mouse over the lower-left corner of the desktop and right-click the **Start** screen thumbnail that appears there. Then, from the context menu that appears, click **Control Panel**.

9. When the *Control Panel* opens, click **System and Security > BitLocker Drive Encryption**. The *BitLocker Drive Encryption* control panel application appears (see Figure 20-1).

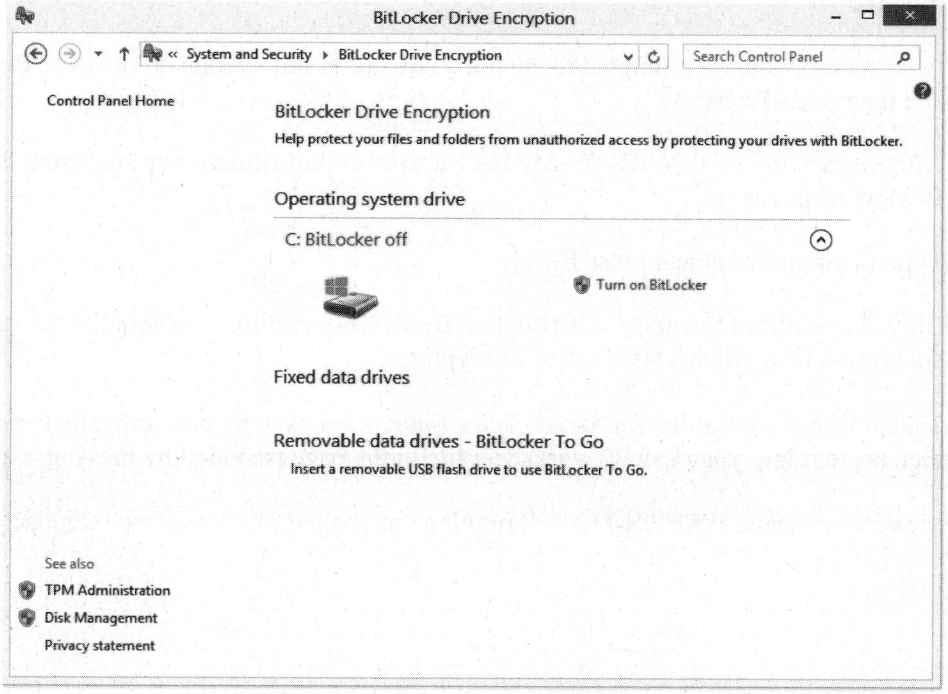

Figure 20-1
The *BitLocker Drive Encryption* page

10. For the *C* drive, click **Turn on BitLocker**.

11. When prompted to choose how you will unlock your drive at startup, click **Enter a password**.

Question 1	*Why is it necessary to use a password to unlock the drive?*

12. In the *Enter your password* text box and in the *Reenter your password* text box, type **Pa$$w0rd** and then click **Next**.

13. When prompted to back up your recovery key, click **Save to a file**

14. Type **SVR-DC-A\Downloads**\ in front of the filename, and then press the **Enter**. Click **Save**.

15. Back on the *How do you want to back up your recovery key?* page, click **Next**.

16. On the *Choose how much of your drive to encrypt* page, click **Next**. On the *Are you ready to encrypt this drive?* page, with *Run BitLocker system check* selected, click **Continue**.

17. Move mouse to lower right corner and select **Settings**. Click **Power** and then click **Restart**.

18. After reboot, you are prompted to enter a password to unlock this drive. Type **Pa$$w0rd** and then press **Enter**.

19. After restart, log on to **WKSTN-MBR-C** as **adatum\administrator** and using the **Pa$$w0rd** password.

20. Type **Control Panel** and press **Enter**.

21. Click **System and Security > BitLocker Drive Encryption**. You should now see the encryption is in process (BitLocker Encrypting).

22. Take a screen shot of the *BitLocker Drive Encryption* page by pressing **Alt+Prt Scr** and then paste it into your Lab 20 worksheet file in the page provided by pressing **Ctrl+V**.

End of exercise. Leave WKSTN-MBR-C running and logged in for the next exercise.

Exercise 20.2	Creating a Data Recovery Agent (DRA)
Overview	In this exercise, you will create an EFS data recovery agent that can be used to recover documents that are protected with EFS.
Mindset	When a user forgets his or her password to unlock a drive that is protected by BitLocker or when a user has left the company and the account has been deleted, a Data Recovery Agent (DRA) can be used to recover the encrypted disk.
Completion time	30 minutes

First, you must install a Certificate Authority by performing the following steps:

1. On **SVR-DC-A**, log on using the **adatum\administrator** account and the **Pa$$w0rd** password.
2. When *Server Manager* opens, click **Manage > Add Roles and Features**.
3. Click **Next** to start the *Add Roles and Features* Wizard.
4. Click **Next** to accept the *Role-based or feature-based installation* default setting.
5. From the *Server* pool, click your domain controller and then click **Next**.
6. On the *Select server roles* page, click to select **Active Directory Certificate Services** and then click **Add Features** to include the management tools.
7. Click **Next** to continue.
8. Click **Next** to continue on the *Select features* screen.
9. After reading the information provided on the *Active Directory Certificate Services* screen, click **Next**.
10. Confirm that *Certification Authority* is checked and then click **Next**.
11. On the *Confirm installation selections* screen, select **Restart the destination server automatically if required** and then click **Yes** to allow automatic restarts.
12. Click **Install** to begin the installation of the AD CS role.
13. When the installation has completed, click **Close**.
14. Click the yellow triangle with black exclamation point that appears at the top of the *Server Manager Dashboard* (see Figure 20-2), and then click **Configure Active Directory Certificate Services on the destination server** to complete the post-deployment configuration.

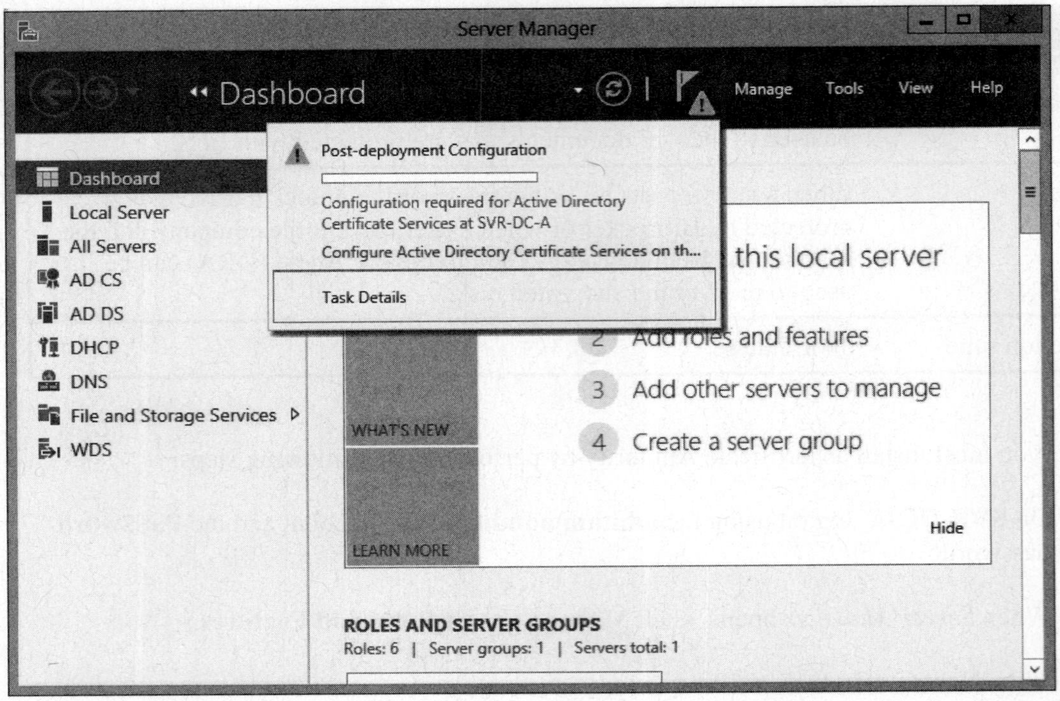

Figure 20-2
The *Post-deployment Configuration* dialog box.

15. On the *Specify credentials to configure role services* screen, click **Next** to accept the default credentials (**ADATUM\Administrator**).

16. On the *Select Role Services to configure* screen, select **Certification Authority** and then click **Next**.

17. On the *Specify the setup type of the CA* screen, click **Next** to accept the *Enterprise CA* default setting.

18. On the *Specify the type of the CA* screen, click **Next** to accept the *Root CA* default setting.

19. On the *Specify the type of the private key* screen, click **Next** to accept the *Create a new private key* default setting.

20. On the *Specify the cryptographic options* screen, click **Next** to accept the default settings.

21. On the *Specify the name of the CA* screen, click **Next** to accept the default settings.

22. On the *Specify the validity period* screen, change the validity period to **10** years. Click **Next** to accept the default settings.

23. On the *Specify the database locations* screen, click **Next** to accept the default settings.

24. Click **Configure**. When the configuration succeeds, click **Close**.

Next, you must request a Digital Certificate by performing the following steps:

1. On **WKSTN-MBR-C**, mouse over the lower-left corner of the desktop and right-click the **Start** screen thumbnail that appears there. Click **Run**.

2. In the *Run* dialog box, type **certmgr.msc**.

3. Click the **Personal Folder**, then right-click the **Personal Folder**, and click **All Tasks > Request New Certificate**.

4. When the *Certificate Enrollment* Wizard appears, click **Next**.

5. Make sure *Active Directory Enrollment Policy* is highlighted and then click **Next** to continue.

6. On the *Request Certificates* screen, select **Basic EFS** and then click **Enroll**.

7. After you are informed the certificate has been enrolled and installed on the computer, click **Finish**.

8. Expand the *Personal* folder, click **Certificates,** and then double-click the **Administrator** certificate.

9. When the *Certificate* dialog box opens, click the **Details** tab.

10. Click the **Copy to File** button. When the *Certificate Export* Wizard dialog box appears, click **Next**.

11. Leave the *No, do not export the private key* option selected and then click **Next**.

12. Verify that the *DER encoded binary X.509 (.CER)* format is selected and then click **Next**.

13. On the *File to Export* page, click **Browse** to display the *Save as* dialog box.

14. In the *File name* text box, type **BitLocker**. In the *Save as type* option, verify that *DER Encoded Binary X.509 (.cer)* is selected and then click **Save**.

Question 2	*What is the path of the certificate export?*

15. Back on the *File to Export* page, click **Next**.

16. Click **Finish** to complete the *Certificate Export* Wizard.

17. Take a screen shot of the *The export was successful* dialog box by pressing **Alt+Prt Scr** and then paste it into your Lab 20 worksheet file in the page provided by pressing **Ctrl+V**.

18. When the *The export was successful* dialog box displays, click **OK**.

19. Close any open dialog boxes.

20. Close the *certmgr* console.

21. Log off of **SVR-DC-A**.

End of exercise. Leave WKSTN-MBR-C running and logged in for the next exercise.

Exercise 20.3	Disabling the Windows Location Provider (WLP)
Overview	In this exercise, you will disable the Windows Location Provider (WLP) for a computer running Windows 8, and then modify a policy to perform the same action.
Mindset	The Windows Location Provider (WLP) is used by applications to gain access to location data. If you do not want to establish location information, you can disable the WLP.
Completion time	10 minutes

1. On **WKSTN-DOM-C**, mouse over the lower-left corner of the desktop and right-click the **Start** screen thumbnail that appears there. Click **Control Panel**.

2. When the *Control Panel* is open, click the **Hardware and Sound** category.

3. Click **Location Settings**.

Question 3	*What does Windows Location Provider use to determine geographic location?*

4. Deselect **Turn on the Windows Location platform** and then click **Apply**.

5. Take a screen shot of the *Location Settings* page by pressing **Alt+Prt Scr** and then paste it into your Lab 20 worksheet file in the page provided by pressing **Ctrl+V**.

6. Close the **Control Panel**.

7. Mouse over the lower-left corner of the desktop and right-click the **Start** screen thumbnail that appears there. Click **Run**.

8. In the *Run* dialog box, type **gpedit.msc**.

9. Click **Computer Configuration > Administrative Templates > Windows Components > Location and Sensors > Windows Location Provider** (see Figure 20-3).

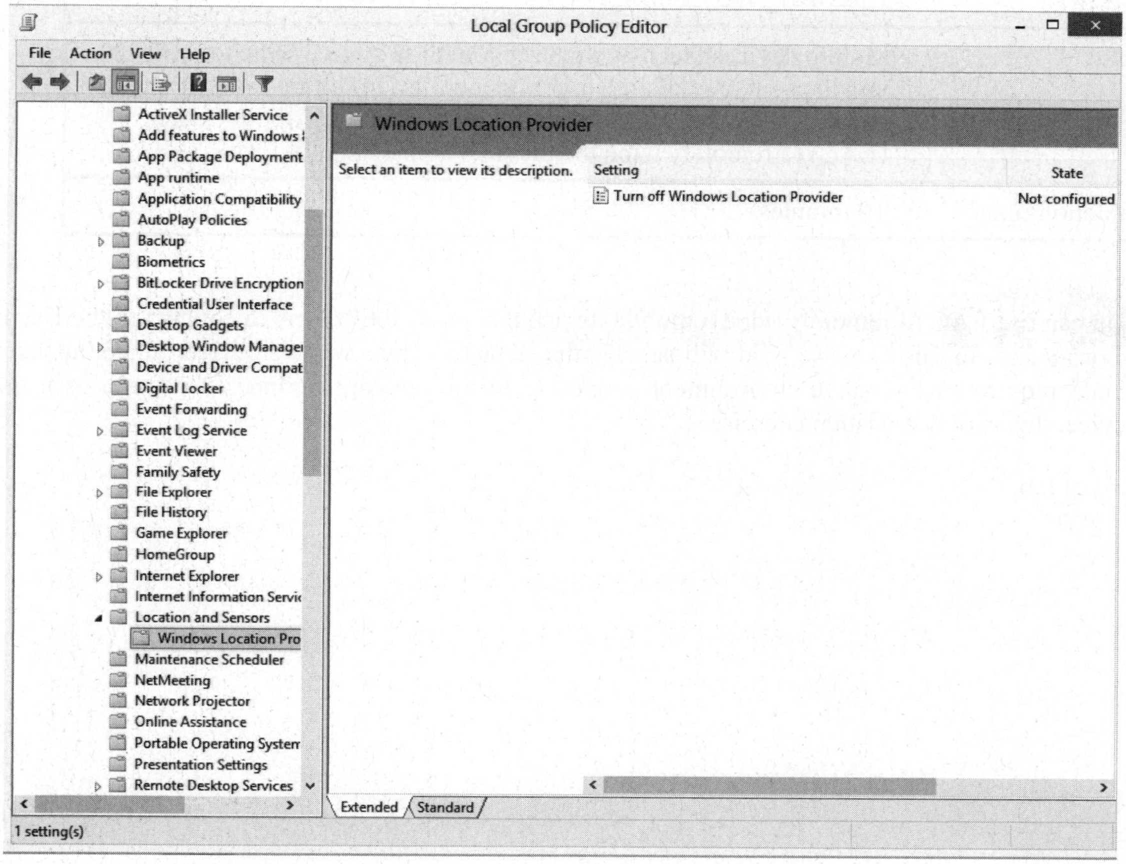

Figure 20-3
The *Windows Location Provider* page

10. Double-click **Turn off Windows Location Provider** and then click **Enabled**.

11. Take a screen shot of the *Turn off Location Provider* dialog box by pressing **Alt+Prt Scr** and then paste it into your Lab 20 worksheet file in the page provided by pressing **Ctrl+V**.

12. Click **OK** to close the *Turn off Windows Location Provider* dialog box.

13. Close **Local Group Policy Editor**.

14. Log off of **WKSTN-MBR-C**.

End of exercise. Close all windows before you start the next exercise.

Lab Challenge	Performing a Remote Wipe using the Exchange Admin Center (EAC)
Overview	In this challenge, you will demonstrate how to perform a remote wipe using the Exchange Admin Center (EAC)
Mindset	Mobile devices (such as a smartphone) use Active Sync to retrieve emails, contacts, and other confidential information. If the phone has become lost or stolen, you can use the Exchange Admin Center (EAC) to remotely wipe the phone.
Completion time	10 minutes

You can use EAC to remotely wipe a mobile device that uses ActiveSync to connect to the Exchange environment. In this exercise, you will specify the steps to wipe a mobile device. Since this exercise would require an Exchange environment connected to the network or Internet as well as a mobile device, this is only a written exercise.

End of lab.

LAB 21
CONFIGURING AND MANAGING UPDATES

THIS LAB CONTAINS THE FOLLOWING EXERCISES AND ACTIVITIES:

Exercise 21.1 Changing Update Settings from the Control Panel

Exercise 21.2 Configuring Windows Update Policies

Exercise 21.3 Uninstalling an Installed Update

Lab Challenge Managing Update settings with GPOs

BEFORE YOU BEGIN

The lab environment consists of student workstations connected to a local area network, along with a server that functions as the domain controller for a domain called adatum.com. The computers required for this lab are listed in Table 21-1.

Table 21-1
Computers Required for Lab 21

Computer	***Operating System***	***Computer Name***
Server	Windows Server 2012	SVR-DC-A
Client	Windows 8 Enterprise	WKSTN-MBR-B

In addition to the computers, you will also need the software listed in Table 21-2 to complete Lab 21.

Table 21-2
Software Required for Lab 21

Software	*Location*
A patch for Internet Explorer 10 (Windows8-RT-KB2761465-x64)	\\svr-dc-a\downloads
Lab 21 student worksheet	Lab21_worksheet.docx (provided by instructor)

Working with Lab Worksheets

Each lab in this manual requires that you answer questions, shoot screen shots, and perform other activities that you will document in a worksheet named for the lab, such as Lab21_worksheet.docx. You will find these worksheets on the book companion site. It is recommended that you use a USB flash drive to store your worksheets so you can submit them to your instructor for review. As you perform the exercises in each lab, open the appropriate worksheet file, type the required information, and then save the file to your flash drive.

SCENARIO

After completing this lab, you will be able to:

- Configure Windows updates
- Install and uninstall an update
- Configure Windows updates using a local policy

Estimated lab time: 55 minutes

Exercise 21.1	Changing Update Settings from the Control Panel
Overview	In this exercise, you will use the Control Panel to configure Windows updates.
Mindset	Unless you use Group Policy (which is often the solution used within larger organizations) to manage Windows updates, you must use the Control Panel to manage Windows update settings.
Completion time	10 minutes

1. On **WKSTN-MBR-B**, log using the **adatum\administrator** account and the **Pa$$w0rd** password.

2. Type **Control Panel** and then select it from the results list.

3. Within the *Control Panel* window, click **System and Security**.

4. To display the *Windows Update* configuration window, click **Windows Update**.

5. On the *Windows Update* page (see Figure 21-1), click **Change settings**. The *Choose your Windows Update settings* window displays.

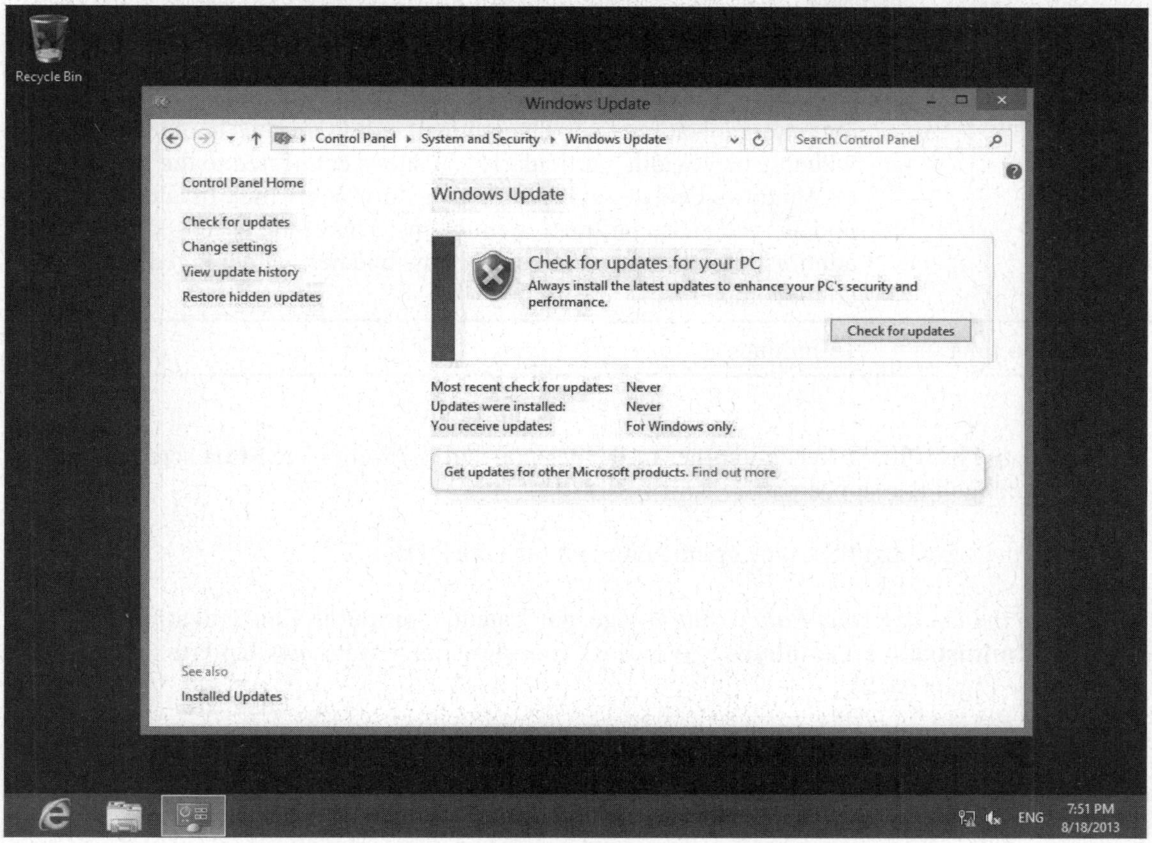

Figure 21-1
The *Windows Update* page

6. Under *Important updates*, click the drop-down and choose **Download updates but let me chose whether to install them**.

Question 1	*Which settings are available for Important updates?*

7. Verify the **Give me recommended updates the same way I receive important updates** option is selected.

8. Take a screen shot of the *Change settings* window by pressing **Alt+Prt Scr** and then paste it into your Lab 21 worksheet file in the page provided by pressing **Ctrl+V**.

9. Click **Cancel** and then close **Windows Update**.

End of exercise. Leave WKSTN-MBR-B running and logged in for the next exercise.

Exercise 21.2	Configuring Windows Update Policies
Overview	In this exercise, you will use Local Group Policy to configure Windows update settings.
Mindset	For an organization, one person downloading updates could waste valuable bandwidth, particularly if a site is connected to the Internet or Windows Update server through a slow WAN link. In addition, updates can cause unforeseen problems. Therefore, as an administrator, you need to control how updates get deployed to client computers.
Completion time	15 minutes

1. Mouse over the lower-left corner of the desktop and right-click the **Start** screen thumbnail that appears there. Click **Run**.

2. In the *Open* text box, type **gpedit.msc** and then click **OK**.

3. On the *Local Group Policy Editor* page, navigate to **Computer Configuration > Administrative Templates > Windows Components > Windows Update** (see Figure 21-2).

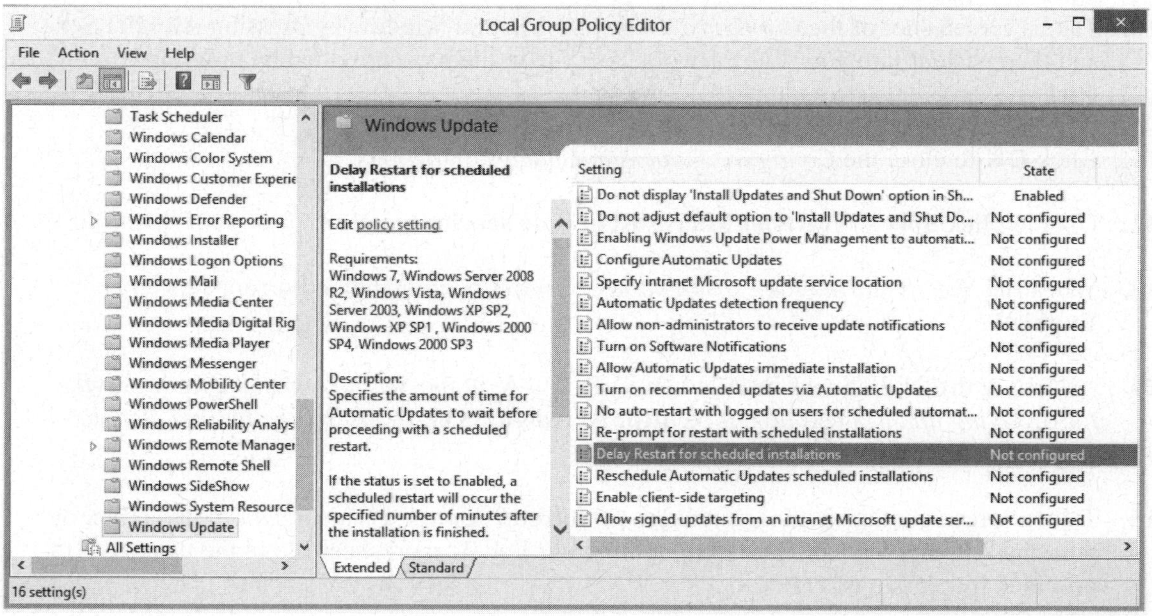

Figure 21-2
Windows Update settings

4. Double-click the **Do not display 'Install Updates and Shut Down' option in Shut Down Windows dialog box**.

5. When the *Do not display 'Install Updates and Shut Down' option in Shut Down Windows dialog box* appears, click **Enabled**.

6. Click **OK** to close the **Do not display 'Install Updates and Shut Down' option in Shut Down Windows** dialog box.

7. Double-click **Configure Automatic Updates**.

8. When the *Configure Automatic Updates* dialog box opens, click **Enabled**.

Question 2	*Which default Configure automatic updating setting is selected?*

Question 3	*By default, when are updates installed?*

9. Change the scheduled install day to **7 - Every Saturday**.

10. Take a screen shot of the *Configure Automatic Updates* window by pressing **Alt+Prt Scr** and then paste it into your Lab 21 worksheet file in the page provided by pressing **Ctrl+V**.

11. Click **OK** to close the *Configure Automatic Updates* dialog box.

12. Double-click **Specify intranet Microsoft update service location**.

13. When the *Specify intranet Microsoft update service location* dialog box appears, click **Enabled**.

14. Assuming that WSUS was installed on SVR-DC-A, in the *Set the intranet update service for detecting updates* text box, type **http://svr-dc-a:8530**. In the *Set the inranet statistics server* text box, type **http://svr-dc-a:8530**.

15. Take a screen shot of the *Specify intranet Microsoft update service location* dialog box by pressing **Alt+Prt Scr** and then paste it into your Lab 21 worksheet file in the page provided by pressing **Ctrl+V**.

16. Click **OK** to close the *Specify intranet Microsoft update service location* dialog box.

17. Double-click **Delay Restart for Scheduled installations**.

18. In the *Delay Restart for scheduled installations* dialog box, click **Enabled**.

19. For the restart (minutes), specify **30** minutes.

Question 4	*If the* Delay Restart for scheduled installations *is not defined, what is the default delay?*

20. Click **OK** to close the *Delay Restart for scheduled installations* dialog box.

21. Close **Local Group Policy Editor**.

End of exercise. Leave WKSTN-MBR-B running and logged in for the next exercise.

Exercise 21.3	Uninstalling an Installed Update
Overview	In this exercise, you will install an update, and then remove the update.
Mindset	If you have a problem with an update and you cannot find an easy solution to fix the problem, you might need to remove the update.
Completion time	20 minutes

1. On **WKSTN-MBR-B**, click the **File Explorer** icon on the Taskbar to open *File Explorer*.
2. Using *File Explorer*, open the **\\SVR-DC-A\Downloads** folder.
3. To install a patch for Internet Explorer 10, double-click **Windows8-RT-KB2761465-x64**.
4. When you are prompted to install the update, click **Yes**.
5. When the update is installed, click **Restart Now**.
6. Log into WKSTN-MBR-B as **adatum\administrator** using **Pa$$w0rd**.
7. Type **Control Panel** and then press **Enter**.
8. When the *Control Panel* opens, click **System and Security > Windows Update**.

Question 5	*If you hide an update that you know you want to install, which option is clicked to view the update?*

9. Click **View update history**.
10. On the *View update history* page, click **Installed Updates**. The updates are listed as shown in Figure 21-3.

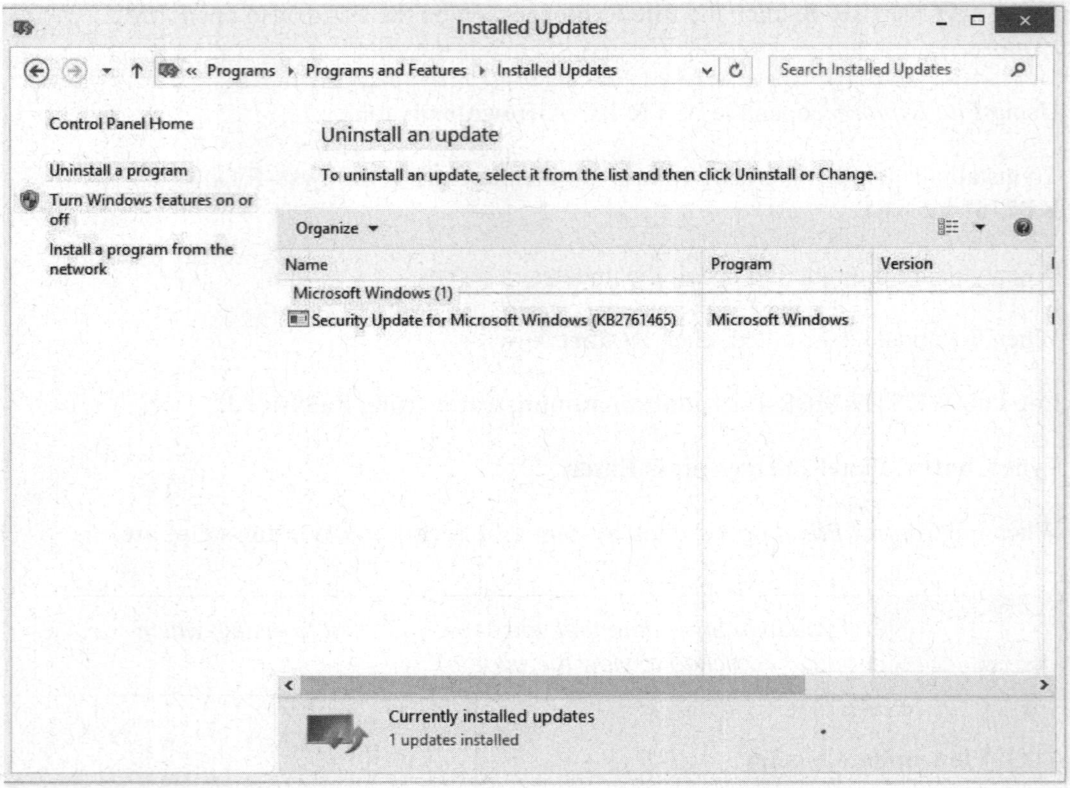

Figure 21-3
The *Installed Updates* page

11. Click **Security Update for Microsoft Windows (KB2761465)** and then click **Uninstall**.
12. When you are prompted to confirm that you want to uninstall this update, click **Yes**.
13. When you are prompted to Restart the computer, take a screen shot by pressing **Alt+Prt Scr** and then paste it into your Lab 21 worksheet file in the page provided by pressing **Ctrl+V**.
14. Click **Restart Now**.

End of exercise. Leave Windows running for the next exercise.

Lab Challenge	Configuring the Do Not Display Install Updates and Shutdown Policy
Overview	During this exercise, you will configure Local Group Policy from a computer running Windows 8.
Mindset	For organizations that manage the updates deployed to users, an administrator might choose not to display that install updates are available to be installed when the computer is being shut down.
Completion time	10 minutes

To complete this challenge, you must have a virtual machine on your computer running Windows 8. You will write out the procedure to configure the *Do not display 'Install Updates and Shut Down' option in Shut Down Windows dialog box* and then take a snapshot of the *Do not display 'Install Updates and Shut Down' option in Shut Down Windows dialog box* page by pressing **Alt+Prt Scr** and then paste the resulting image into the Lab 21 worksheet file in the page provided by pressing **Ctrl+V**.

End of lab.

LAB 22
MANAGING LOCAL STORAGE

THIS LAB CONTAINS THE FOLLOWING EXERCISES AND ACTIVITIES:

Exercise 22.1 Working with Basic Partitions

Exercise 22.2 Working with Dynamic Partitions

Lab Challenge Managing Storage Spaces

BEFORE YOU BEGIN

The lab environment consists of computers connected to a local area network. The computers required for this lab are listed in Table 22-1.

Table 22-1
Computers Required for Lab 22

Computer	*Operating System*	*Computer Name*
Server	Windows Server 2012	SVR-DC-A
Workstation	Windows 8 Enterprise	WKSTN-MBR-B
Workstation	Windows 8 Enterprise	WKSTN-MBR-C

Aside from its system disk, the WKSTN-MBR-C workstation will require two additional disk drives, holding 20 GB each.

In addition to the computers, you will also need the software listed in Table 22-2 to complete Lab 22.

Table 22-2
Software Required for Lab 22

Software	***Location***
Lab 22 student worksheet	Lab22_worksheet.docx (provided by instructor)

Working with Lab Worksheets

Each lab in this manual requires that you answer questions, create screenshots, and perform other activities that you will document in a worksheet named for the lab, such as Lab22_worksheet.docx. You will find these worksheets on the book companion site. It is recommended that you use a USB flash drive to store your worksheets so you can submit them to your instructor for review. As you perform the exercises in each lab, open the appropriate worksheet file, type the required information, and then save the file to your flash drive.

SCENARIO

After completing this lab, you will be able to:

- Create and manipulate volumes on a basic disk
- Create and manipulate volumes on a dynamic disk
- Create and manipulate storage spaces

Estimated lab time: 40 minutes

Exercise 22.1	Working with Basic Partitions
Overview	In this exercise, you will create and manipulate partitions on a basic disk.
Mindset	Basic disks enable you to create simple volumes and then extend or shrink them as needed.
Completion time	10 minutes

1. On **WKSTN-MBR-C**, log on using the **adatum\Administrator** account and the **Pa$$w0rd** password.
2. On the **Start** screen, click the **Desktop** tile. The *Desktop* appears.
3. Mouse over the lower-left corner of the desktop, right-click the **Start** screen thumbnail and, from the context menu, choose **Disk Management**. The *Disk Management* snap-in appears (see Figure 22-1).

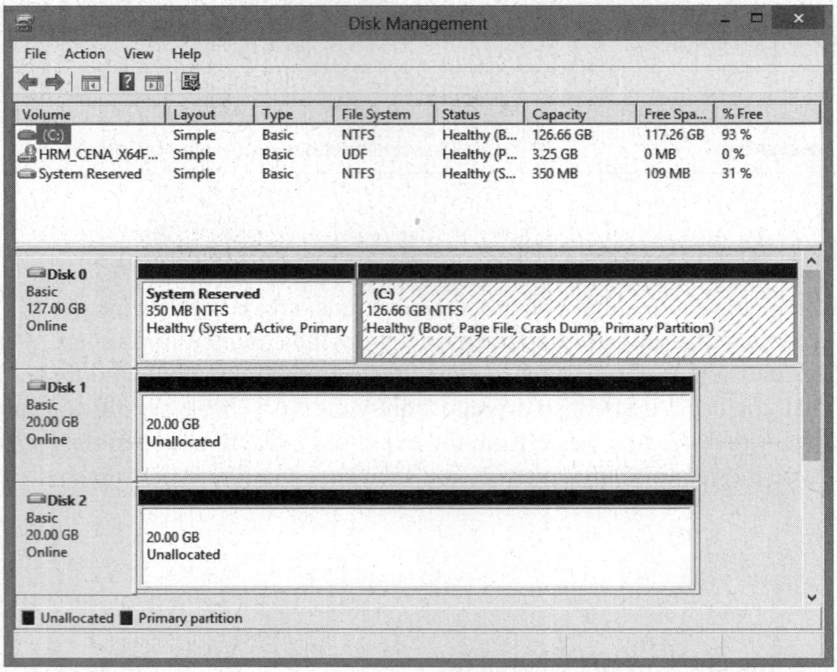

Figure 22-1
The *Disk Management* snap-in

4. Click **OK** to initialize *Disk1* and *Disk2*. Based on the information in the Disk Management snap-in, fill out the information in Table 22-1 on your lab worksheet.

Table 22-1
Disk information

	Disk 0	*Disk 1*	*Disk 2*
Disk type (basic or dynamic)			
Total disk size			
Number and type of partitions			
Amount of unallocated space			

5. In the graphical display of the snap-in, in the *Disk 1* information, right-click the Unallocated area and choose **New Simple Volume**. The *New Simple Volume* Wizard appears.

6. Click **Next** to bypass the *Welcome* page. The *Specify Volume Size* page appears.

7. In the *Simple Volume Size In MB* text box, type **2000** and then click **Next**. The *Assign Drive Letter Or Path* page appears.

8. Leave the *Assign the following drive letter* option selected, choose drive letter **X** from the drop-down list, and then click **Next**. The *Format Partition* page appears.

9. Leave the *Format this volume with the following settings* option selected and then configure the next three parameters as follows:

   - *File System:* **FAT32**
   - *Allocation Unit Size:* **Default**
   - *Volume Label:* **Part1**

10. Leave the *Perform a quick format* check box selected and then click **Next**. The *Completing The New Simple Volume Wizard* page appears.

11. Click **Finish**. The new volume appears in the *Disk Management* window.

12. Take a screen shot of the *Disk Management* window that shows the simple volume you created by pressing **Ctrl+Prt Scr** and then paste the resulting image into the Lab 22 worksheet file in the page provided by pressing **Ctrl+V**.

End of exercise. Leave all windows open for the next exercise.

Exercise 22.2	Working with Dynamic Partitions
Overview	In this exercise, you will create a spanned volume that utilizes space from two physical hard disks.
Mindset	A spanned volume enables you to combine the space from two or more disks into a single entity.
Completion time	10 minutes

1. On **WKSTN-MBR-C**, in the *Disk Management* snap-in, in the graphical display, right-click the **Disk 1** box and choose **Convert To Dynamic Disk**. The *Convert To Dynamic Disk* dialog box appears.

2. Leave the default Disk 1 check box selected and then click **OK**. The *Disks to Convert* dialog box appears (see Figure 22-2).

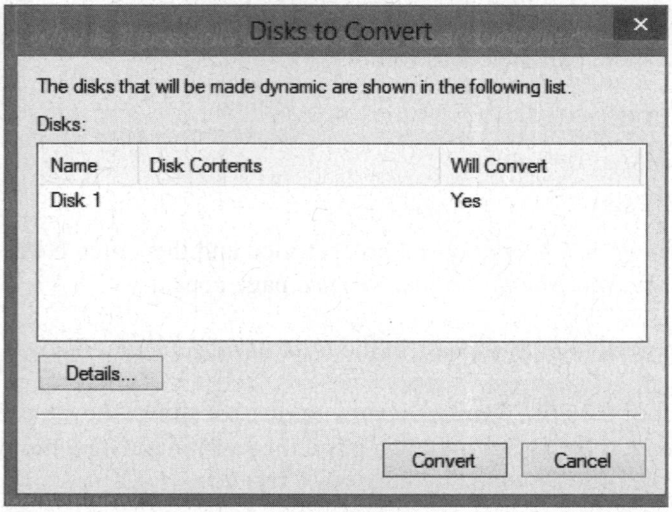

Figure 22-2
The *Disks to Convert* dialog box

3. Click **Convert**. A *Disk Management* message box appears, warning you that after you convert the disk to a dynamic disk, you will not be able to start installed operating systems from any volume other than the current boot volume.

4. Click **Yes** to continue. The program performs the disk conversion.

Question 1	*What has happened to the primary partition you created earlier in this lab?*

Question 2	*After you converted the basic disk to a dynamic disk, how many partitions can be found on the disk? How do you know?*

5. Right-click the **Part1** volume and study the context menu.

Question 3	*Why is the option to extend the volume grayed out?*

6. Right-click the unallocated space on **Disk1** and choose **New Spanned Volume**. The *New Spanned Volume* Wizard appears, displaying the *Welcome* page.

7. Click **Next**. The *Select Disks* page appears.

8. In the *Available* box, select **Disk2** and then click **Add**. *Disk2* moves to the *Selected* box.

9. Using the *Select the amount of space in MB* spin-box, configure *Disk1* and *Disk2* to contribute all of their available disk space to the spanned volume and then click **Next**. The *Assign Drive Letter or Path* page appears.

10. Select the drive letter **Z** and then click **Next**. The *Format Volume* page appears.

11. Leave the *Format this volume with the following settings* option selected and then configure the next three parameters as follows:

    - *File System:* **NTFS**
    - *Allocation Unit Size:* **Default**
    - *Volume Label:* **Part2**

12. Select the *Perform a quick format* check box and click then click **Next**. The *Completing The New Spanned Volume Wizard* page appears.

13. Click **Finish**. Click Yes to convert Disk 2 to dynamic. The wizard creates the volume.

14. Take a screen shot of the *Disk Management* window that shows the spanned volume you created by pressing **Ctrl+Prt Scr** and then paste the resulting image into the Lab 22 worksheet file in the page provided by pressing **Ctrl+V**.

End of exercise. Leave all windows open for the next exercise.

Lab Challenge	Managing Storage Spaces
Overview	In this challenge, you will use storage spaces to create a fault tolerant storage pool on a workstation running Windows 8
Mindset	Windows 8 includes a new storage virtualization technology called Storage Spaces, which enables a computer to use storage space from individual physical disks to create a virtual disk.
Completion time	20 minutes

To complete this challenge, you must delete the volumes you created on Disk1 and Disk2 of WKSTN-MBR-C and then use those disks to create a storage pool and a storage space with the following parameters:

- *Name:* **Databases**
- *Drive Letter:* **P**
- *Resiliency type:* **Two-way mirror**
- *Maximum size:* **80 GB**

Write out the steps you followed to complete the challenge and then show the pool you created by using **Ctrl+Prt Scr** to take screen shots of the *Create a storage pool* dialog box, the *Create a storage space* dialog box, and the *Disk Management* window. Then paste the resulting images into the Lab 22 worksheet file in the page provided by pressing **Ctrl+V**.

End of lab.

LAB 23
MONITORING SYSTEM PERFORMANCE

THIS LAB CONTAINS THE FOLLOWING EXERCISES AND ACTIVITIES:

BEFORE YOU BEGIN

The lab environment consists of student workstations connected to a local area network, along with a server that functions as the domain controller for a domain called adatum.com. The computers required for this lab are listed in Table 23-1.

Table 23-1
Computers Required for Lab 23

Computer	*Operating System*	*Computer Name*
Server	Windows Server 2012	SVR-DC-A
Client	Windows 8 Enterprise	WKSTN-MBR-B

In addition to the computers, you will also need the software listed in Table 23-2 to complete Lab 23.

Table 23-2
Software Required for Lab 23

Software	***Location***
Lab 23 student worksheet	Lab23_worksheet.docx (provided by instructor)

Working with Lab Worksheets

Each lab in this manual requires that you answer questions, shoot screen shots, and perform other activities that you will document in a worksheet named for the lab, such as Lab23_worksheet.docx. You will find these worksheets on the book companion site. It is recommended that you use a USB flash drive to store your worksheets, so you can submit them to your instructor for review. As you perform the exercises in each lab, open the appropriate worksheet file, type the required information, and then save the file to your flash drive.

SCENARIO

After completing this lab, you will be able to:

- View Windows logs using Event Viewer
- View performance using Task Manager, Resource Manager, and Performance Monitor
- Use Reliability Monitor for potential problems

Estimated lab time: 80 minutes

Exercise 23.1	Using Event Viewer
Overview	In this exercise, you will use the Event Viewer to look at the current Windows logs and to create a filter so that you can reduce the number of entries.
Mindset	The Event Viewer is used to view the warnings and errors for Windows.
Completion time	10 minutes

1. On **WKSTN-MBR-B**, log on using the **Adatum\administrator** account and the **Pa$$w0rd** password.
2. Type **Administrative Tools** and then press **Enter**.
3. When the *Administrative Tools* window opens, double-click **Event Viewer**.

4. Expand the **Windows Logs** folder and then click the **System** log (see Figure 23-1). The contents of the log appear in the detail pane.

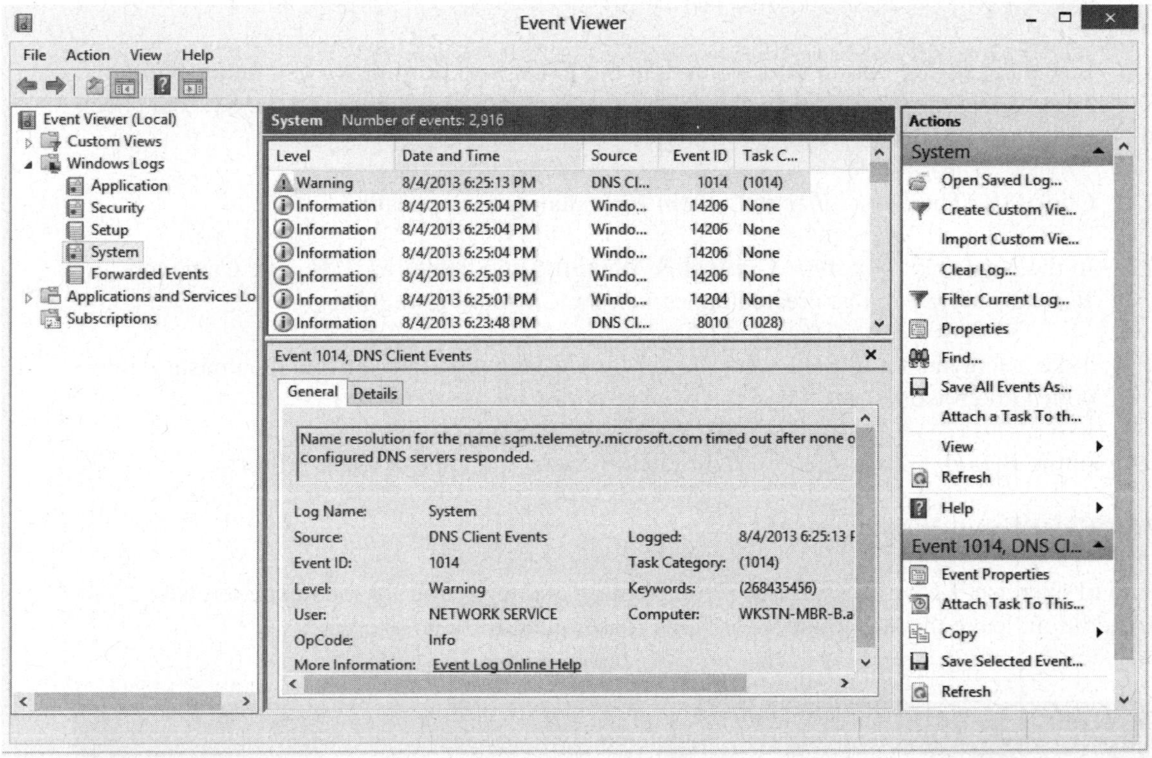

Figure 23-1
The *Event Viewer* page

Question 1	*How many events appear in the System log?*

5. Click the **Action** menu and choose **Filter Current Log**. The *Filter Current Log* dialog box appears.

6. In the *Event Level* area, select the **Critical** check box and then select the **Warning** check box. Click **OK**.

Question 2	*How many events appear in the System log now?*

7. Click **Action** > **Create Custom View**. The *Create Custom View* dialog box appears.

8. In the *Logged* drop-down list, click **Last 7 days**.

9. In the *Event Level* area, click the **Critical** check box and then select the **Warning** check box.

10. Leave the *By log* option selected and, in the *Event logs* drop-down list, under *Windows Logs*, select the **Application** check box, the **Security** check box, and the **System** check box.

11. Click **OK**. The *Save Filter to Custom View* dialog box appears.

12. In the *Name* text box, type **Critical & Warning** and then click **OK**. The *Critical & Warning* view you just created appears in the *Custom Views* folder.

13. Take a screen shot of the Event Viewer by pressing **Alt+Prt Scr** and then paste it into your Lab 23 worksheet file in the page provided by pressing **Ctrl+V**.

14. In the *Windows Logs* section, right-click **System** and choose **Clear Filter**.

15. Close **Event Viewer**.

End of exercise. Leave WKSTN-MBR-B running and logged in for the next exercise. In addition, leave the Administrative Tools folder open for later exercises.

Exercise 23.2	Using Task Manager
Overview	In this exercise, you will use the Task Manager to look at the basic performance of the system and to view the current processes running on Windows.
Mindset	Use the Task Manager when you need to quickly determine how well your machine is performing or when you need to stop a process that will not stop on its own.
Completion time	20 minutes

1. On **WKSTN-MBR-B**, right-click the **Taskbar** and choose **Task Manager**.

Question 3	*Which applications are running?*

Question 4	*Which tabs are shown?*

2. Click **More Details**. *Task Manager* expands (see Figure 23-2).

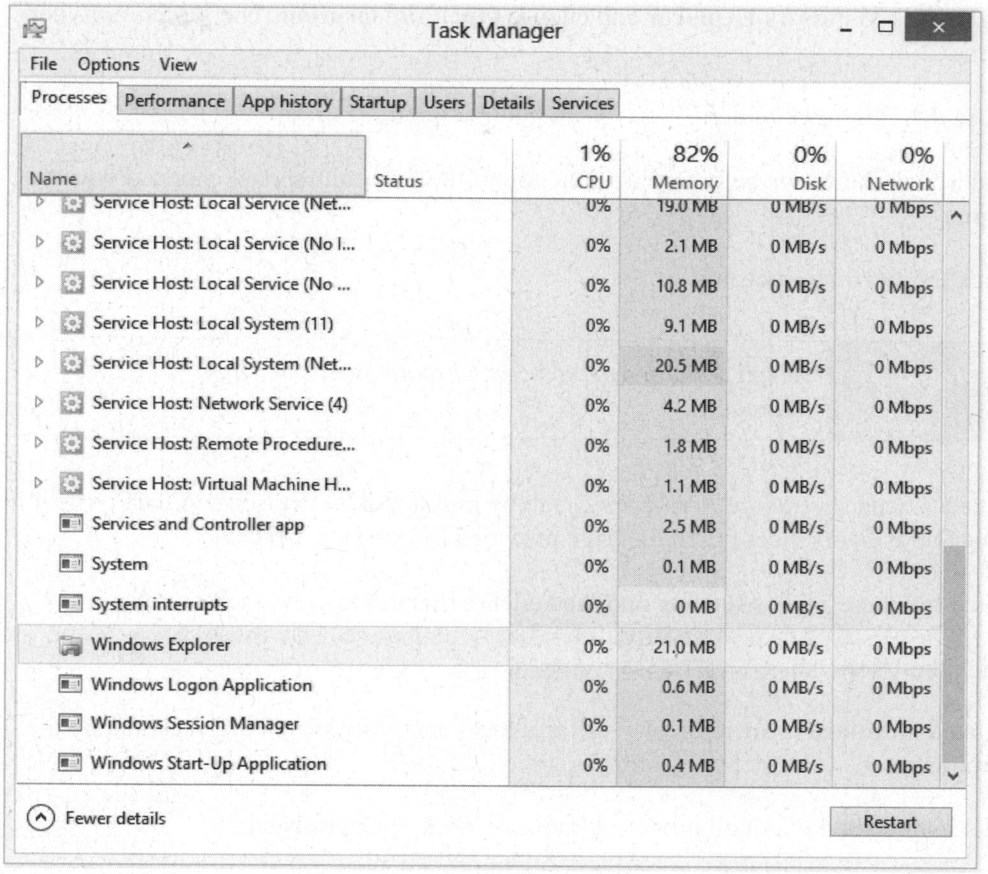

Figure 23-2
The *Task Manager* page

Question 5	*Which tabs are shown?*

3. Mouse over the lower-left corner of the desktop and click the **Start** screen thumbnail that appears there. Type **wordpad** and then press **Enter**.

Question 6	*In the Apps section, which process is used for WordPad?*

4. On the *Task Manager* page, click **Fewer details**.

5. Right-click **Windows Wordpad Application** and choose **End Task**.

6. Click **More details**.

7. Right-click **Windows Explorer** and choose **Open file location**. The *Windows* folder opens.

8. Close the **Windows** folder.

9. Right-click the ***Name*** column title at the top of the first column and choose **Process name**.

10. Click the **Performance** tab.

Question 7	*Which primary systems can be monitored with Task Manager?*

11. Take a screen shot of the *Performance* tab by pressing **Alt+Prt Scr** and then paste it into your Lab 23 worksheet file in the page provided by pressing **Ctrl+V**.

12. In the left pane, click **Memory** and then click **Ethernet** to view each option.

13. Click the **Users** tab.

14. Expand **Administrator** to display the programs and processes being executed by the administrator.

15. To see a detailed list of all processes running, click the **Details** tab.

16. To display additional columns, right-click the **Name** column title and choose **Select columns**.

17. When the *Select columns* dialog box opens, click to select the **Session ID** column and select the **Threads** column. Click **OK**.

18. To sort by components that make up the most memory, click the **Memory (private work set)** title.

19. From time to time, a program or action might cause Windows Explorer to stop functioning. In these cases, you can use Task Manager to stop and restart Explorer. Therefore, find and right-click **explorer.exe** and then choose **End task**.

20. When you are prompted to end *explorer.exe*, click **End process**.

21. Click **File** > **Run new task**.

22. When the *Create new task* dialog box, in the *Open* text box, type **explorer** and then click **OK**.

23. To view the current services, click the **Services** tab.

24. Close **Task Manager**.

End of exercise. Close any open windows before you begin the next exercise.

Exercise 23.3	Using Performance Monitor Console
Overview	In this exercise, you will open the Performance Monitor to take a closer look at system performance.
Mindset	The Task Manager gives you a quick view of system performance, but you can use Performance Monitor to probe a bit deeper (including the use of performance counters).
Completion time	30 minutes

To monitor various performance counters, perform the following steps:

1. On **WKSTN-MBR-B**, using **Administrative Tools**, double-click **Performance Monitor**.

2. Browse to and click **Monitoring Tools\Performance Monitor** (see Figure 23-3).

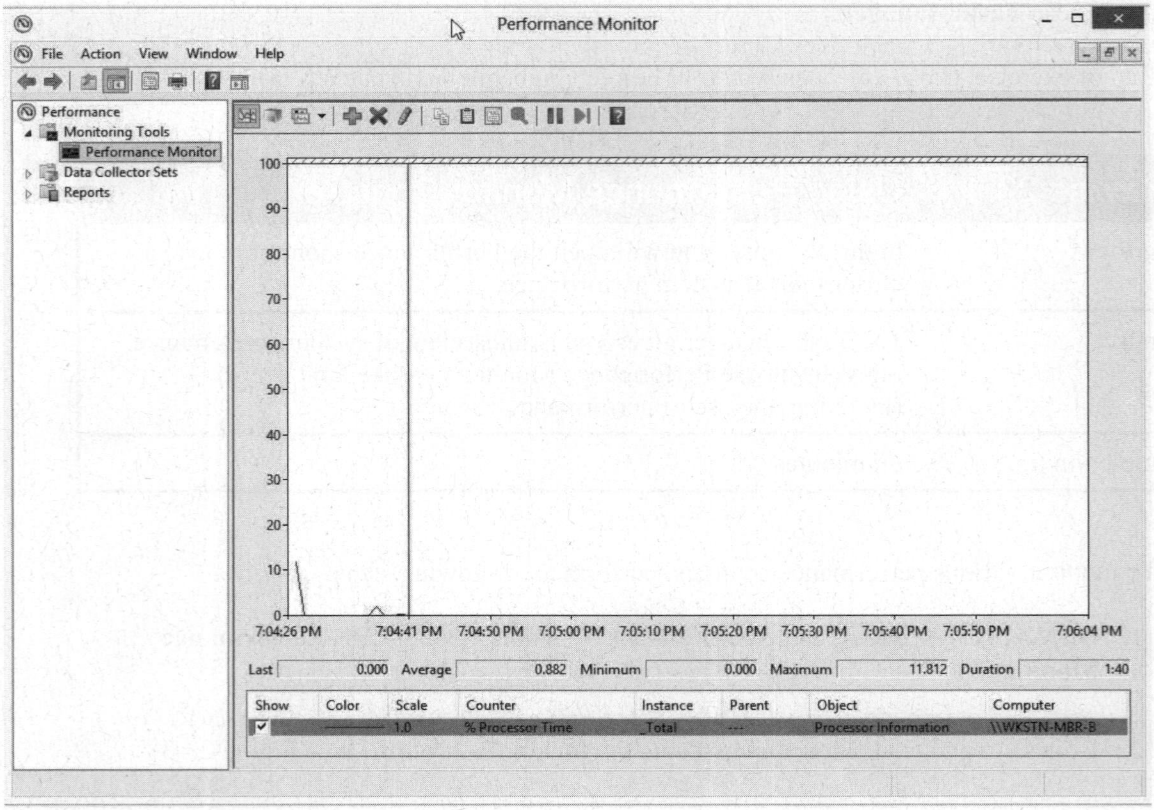

Figure 23-3
The *Performance Monitor* page

3. At the bottom of the screen, click **% Processor Time**. To remove the counter, click the **Delete** (red X) button at the top of the Window.

4. Click the **Add** (green plus (+) sign) button on the Toolbar. The *Add Counters* dialog box appears.

5. Under *Available counters*, expand **Processor**, click **% Processor Time**, and then click **Show description**. Read the description for *% Processor Time*.

6. Click **Add**. *% Processor Time* should show up in the *Added counters* section.

7. Under *Available Counters*, expand the **Server Work Queues** and then click the **Queue Length** counter. Under *Instances of selected objects*, click **0**. Then click **Add**.

8. Add the following counters:

   - *System:* **Processor Queue Length**
   - *Memory:* **Page Faults/Sec**
   - *Memory:* **Pages/Sec**
   - *PhysicalDisk (_Total):* **Current Disk Queue Length**

9. Click **OK** to close the *Add Counters* dialog box.

10. Mouse over the lower-left corner of the desktop, right-click the **Start** screen thumbnail that appears there, and then click **Command Prompt (Admin)**.

11. At the command prompt, execute the following command:

    ```
    dir c:\ /s
    ```

    You should see a spike in CPU usage.

12. At the top of the graph, you see a Toolbar with 13 buttons. Click the down arrow of the **Change graph type** (third button) and then click **Histogram bar**.

13. Change the graph type to **Report**.

14. Change back to the **Line graph**.

15. Click the **Properties** button (the fifth button from the end) on the Toolbar. The *Performance Monitor Properties* sheet appears. Notice the counters that you have selected.

16. Click **Processor (_Total)\%Processor Time**.

17. Change the width to heaviest line width. Change the color to **Red**.

18. Click the **Graph** tab.

19. In the *Vertical scale* box, change the value of the *Maximum* field to **200** and then click **OK**.

20. Close the *Administrator: Command Prompt* window.

To create and use a Data Collector Set, perform the following steps:

1. On **WKSTN-MBR-B**, in the left pane, expand **Data Collector Sets**.

2. Right-click the **User Defined** folder, choose **New** and then click **Data Collector Set**. In the *Name:* text box type **MyDCS1**.

3. Click **Create manually (Advanced)** and then click **Next**.

4. Select **Performance Counter** and then click **Next**.

5. To add counters, click **Add**.

6. Under *Available Counters*, expand the *Processor* node by clicking the down arrow next to *Processor*. Scroll down and click **%Processor Time**. Click **Add**.

7. Add the following counters.
   - *Server Work Queues:* **Queue Length counter**
   - *System:* **Processor Queue Length**
   - *Memory:* **Page Faults/Sec**
   - *Memory:* **Pages/Sec**
   - *PhysicalDisk (_Total):* **Current Disk Queue Length**
8. Click **OK** and then click **Next**.
9. Click **Finish**.
10. Right-click **MyDCS1** and choose **Start**.
11. Let it run for at least two minutes.
12. Right-click **MyDCS1** and choose **Stop**.
13. Open **File Explorer** and navigate to **c:\PerfLogs\Admin\MyDCS1**. Then open the folder that was just created.
14. Double-click **DataCollector01.blg**. The *Performance Monitor* graph opens.

Question 8	*Now that the DCS has been created, what advantages does the MyDCS1 have?*

15. Take a screen shot of the *Performance Monitor* window by pressing **Alt+Prt Scr** and then paste it into your Lab 23 worksheet file in the page provided by pressing **Ctrl+V**.
16. Close the **Performance Monitor** graph and then close the **MyDCS1** folder.
17. Close **Performance Monitor**.

End of exercise. Leave the *Administrator Tools* window open. You can close any other open windows before you begin the next exercise.

Exercise 23.4	Using Resource Monitor
Overview	In this exercise, you will use Resource Monitor to determine which processes are using the primary computer resources.
Mindset	The Resource Monitor extends the capabilities of the Task Manager.
Completion time	10 minutes

1. On **WKSTN-MBR-B**, using the *Administrative Tools*, double-click **Resource Monitor**.

Question 9	*Which primary systems can be monitored with Resource Monitor?*

2. On the *Resource Monitor* page (see Figure 23-4), click the **CPU** tab.

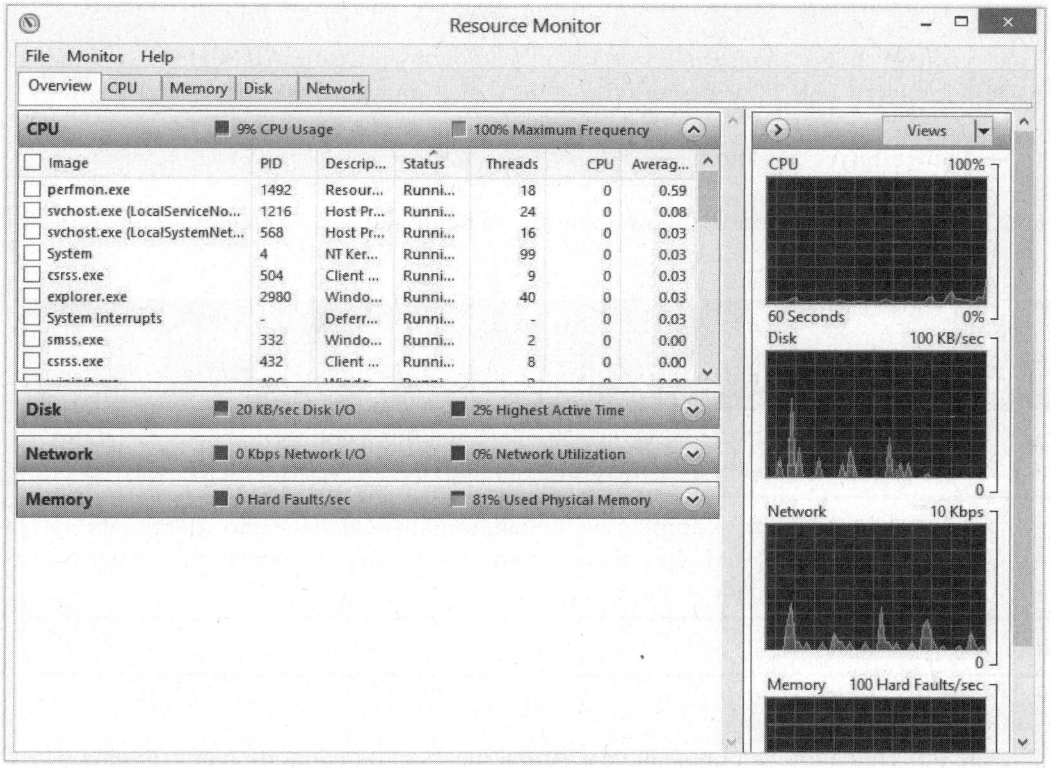

Figure 23-4
The *Resource Monitor* page

3. To sort the processes alphabetically, click the **Image** title at the top of the first column in the *Processes* section.

4. Click the **Memory** tab.

Question 10	*Which process is using the most memory?*

5. Click the **Disk** tab.

Question 11	*Which process is using the disk the most?*

6. Click the **Network** tab and then expand **Listening Ports**.

Question 12	*Which image is listening on port 53?*

7. Take a screen shot of the *Resource Monitor* window by pressing **Alt+Prt Scr** and then paste it into your Lab 23 worksheet file in the page provided by pressing **Ctrl+V**.

8. Close the **Resource Monitor**.

End of exercise. Close any open windows before you begin the next exercise.

Lab Challenge	Using Reliability Monitor
Overview	In this exercise, you will open the Reliability Monitor to check the status of the computer by generating a system health report.
Mindset	The Reliability Monitor is a hidden tool that can determine the reliability of a system, including allowing you to see whether any recent changes have been made to the system itself
Completion time	10 minutes

To complete this challenge, you must have a virtual machine on your computer running Windows 8. You will write out the procedure to open Reliability Monitor and generate a system health report. Then you will take a snapshot of the *Resource and Performance Monitor System Diagnostics Report* page by pressing **Alt+Prt Scr** and then paste the resulting image into the Lab 23 worksheet file in the page provided by pressing **Ctrl+V**.

End of lab.

LAB 24 CONFIGURING BACKUPS

THIS LAB CONTAINS THE FOLLOWING EXERCISES AND ACTIVITIES:

BEFORE YOU BEGIN

The lab environment consists of computers connected to a local area network in an Active Directory Domain Services configuration. The computers required for this lab are listed in Table 24-1.

Table 24-1
Computers Required for Lab 24

Computer	*Operating System*	*Computer Name*
Server	Windows Server 2012	SVR-DC-A
Workstation	Windows 8 Enterprise	WKSTN-MBR-B
Workstation	Windows 8 Enterprise	WKSTN-MBR-C

In addition to the computers, you will also need the software listed in Table 24-2 to complete Lab 24.

Table 24-2
Software Required for Lab 24

Software	*Location*
Lab 24 student worksheet	Lab24_worksheet.docx (provided by instructor)

Working with Lab Worksheets

Each lab in this manual requires that you answer questions, create screenshots, and perform other activities that you will document in a worksheet named for the lab, such as Lab24_worksheet.docx. You will find these worksheets on the book companion site. It is recommended that you use a USB flash drive to store your worksheets so you can submit them to your instructor for review. As you perform the exercises in each lab, open the appropriate worksheet file, type the required information, and then save the file to your flash drive.

SCENARIO

After completing this lab, you will be able to:

- Create backup jobs
- Understand incremental backup jobs
- Create a backup schedule

Estimated lab time: 45 minutes

Exercise 24.1	Creating a Custom Backup Job
Overview	In this exercise, you will use the Windows 7 File Recovery program to back up files on a Windows 8 computer.
Mindset	Windows 8 includes the backup program from Windows 7 to support users with existing backups made with the previous operating system version.
Completion time	20 minutes

1. On **WKSTN-MBR-C**, log on using the **adatum\Administrator** account and the **Pa$$w0rd** password.
2. Click the **Desktop** tile. The *Desktop* appears.
3. Mouse over the lower-left corner of the desktop and right-click the **Start** screen thumbnail that appears there. Then, from the context menu that appears, click **Disk Management**. The *Disk Management* window appears.

4. On Disk 1, right-click the unallocated space and choose **New Simple Volume**. The *New Simple Volume* Wizard appears.

5. Follow the instructions in the wizard to create an NTFS volume from all of the unallocated disk space using the drive letter **X:** and the volume name **Backup**.

6. Close the *Disk Management* window.

7. Mouse over the lower-left corner of the desktop and right-click the **Start** screen thumbnail that appears there. Then, from the context menu that appears, click **Control Panel**. The *Control Panel* window appears.

8. In the *View by* drop-down list, click **Large icons**. The *Control Panel* interface displays individual icons for each of the available applications.

9. Click **Windows 7 File Recovery**. The *Windows 7 File Recovery* control panel appears (see Figure 24-1).

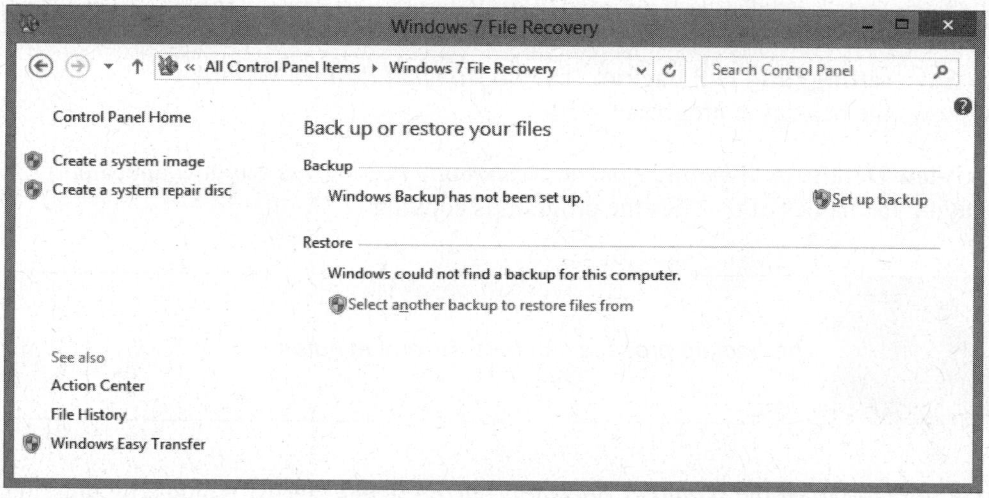

Figure 24-1
The *Windows 7 File Recovery* control panel

10. Click **Set up backup**. The *Set Up Backup* Wizard appears, displaying the *Select where you want to save your backup* page.

11. Select the **Backup (X:)** partition and then click Next. The *What do you want to back up?* page appears.

Question 1	*Why doesn't the system drive (C:) appear on the* Select where you want to save your backup *page?*

12. Select the **Let me choose** option and then click **Next**. The *What do you want to back up?* page appears.

13. Expand the **Local Disk (C:)** container.

Question 2	*Why doesn't the Windows folder appear under the Local Disk (C:) drive?*

14. Select the **Local Disk (C:)** check box and then clear the **Include a system image of drives: System Reserved, (C:)** check box. Click **Next**. The *Review your backup settings* page appears.

15. Click **Change Schedule**. The *How often do you want to back up?* page appears.

16. Clear the **Run backup on a schedule (recommended)** check box and then click **OK**. The schedule indicator on the *Review your backup settings* page changes to *On demand.*

17. Take a screen shot of the *Review your backup settings* page by pressing **Alt+Prt Scr** and then paste the resulting image into the Lab 24 worksheet file in the page provided by pressing **Ctrl+V**.

18. Click **Save settings and run backup**. The *Backup and Restore* Wizard now shows the backup in progress.

19. Click **View Details**. A *Windows Backup is currently in progress* window appears, displaying the names of the files the program is copying.

NOTE	*The backup process can take several minutes.*

20. Take a screen shot of the *Windows Backup is currently in progress* window by pressing **Alt+Prt Scr** and then paste the resulting image into the Lab 24 worksheet file in the page provided by pressing **Ctrl+V**.

21. Click **Close**.

Question 3	*What is the size of the backup, as indicated on the Backup and Restore control panel?*

22. Close the *Windows 7 File Recovery* control panel.

End of exercise. Close all open windows before the next exercise.

Exercise 24.2	Performing an Incremental Backup Job
Overview	In this exercise, you will create a new file on the computer and repeat the backup job you performed in Exercise 24.1 to demonstrate how incremental backup jobs work.
Mindset	An incremental backup job only saves the files that have changed since the last backup. This saves time and storage space on the backup medium.
Completion time	15 minutes

1. On **WKSTN-MBR-C**, mouse over the lower-left corner of the desktop and right-click the **Start** screen thumbnail that appears there.

2. On the **Start** screen, type **Notepad**. Then, in the results area, click the *Notepad* tile. A *Notepad* window appears (see Figure 24-2).

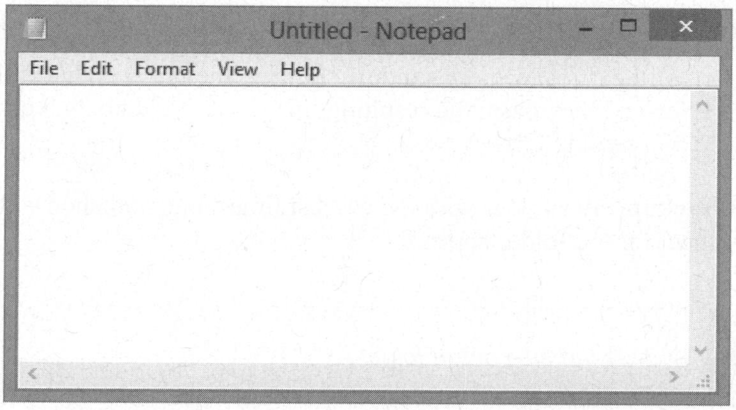

Figure 24-2
A *Notepad* window

3. Type any text in the Notepad window and then click **File** > **Save As**. The *Save As* combo box appears.

4. In the *File name* text box, type **c:\newfile.txt** and then click **Save**. Notepad creates the new file at the root of the C: drive.

5. Open the **Windows 7 File Recovery** control panel, just as you did in Exercise 24.1.

Question 4	*How is the Windows 7 control panel interface different from when you opened it the first time?*

6. Click **Back up now**. The program repeats the backup job you configured earlier.

Question 5	*How does the time required for this backup compare with that for the same job the first time you ran it?*

7. Switch to the **Notepad** window.

8. Modify the text you typed in the *Notepad* window and then click **File** > **Save**.

9. Switch back to the **Windows 7 File Recovery** control panel and then click **Back up now** again. The program performs a third backup.

10. On the Taskbar, click the **File Explorer** button. A *File Explorer* window appears.

11. Browse to the **Backup (X:)** drive, expand the **WKSTN-MBR-C** container and expand the folder beginning with **Backup Set** (including the date).

Question 6	*How many Backup Files folders are there beneath the Backup Set folder?*

12. Take a screen shot of the *File Explorer* window showing the *Backup Files* folders, by pressing **Alt+Prt Scr** and then paste the resulting image into the Lab 24 worksheet file in the page provided by pressing **Ctrl+V**.

13. Right-click the **Backup Files** folder with the earliest timestamp and choose **Properties**. The *Properties* sheet for the folder appears.

Question 7	*What is the size of the folder?*

14. Click **OK** to close the *Properties* sheet.

15. Open the *Properties* sheet for the second and third *Backup Files* folders.

Question 8	*Why are these Backup Files folders so much smaller than the first one?*

16. Click **OK** to close the Properties sheet.

End of exercise. Leave all windows open for the next exercise.

Lab Challenge	Scheduling a Backup Job
Overview	Performing a single backup job provides only limited protection against hardware failure. To fully protect your data, you must back up regularly. Windows 8 enables you to schedule backup jobs to run at specified intervals.
Mindset	Creating a regularly scheduled backup strategy is an essential part of Windows 8 administration.
Completion time	10 minutes

To complete this challenge, you must create a job that backs up your workstation's entire system (C:) drive to the X: drive every Friday at 11:00 PM. Write out the procedure for creating the job and take a screen shot of the *Review your backup settings* page by pressing **Alt+Prt Scr** and then paste the resulting image into the Lab 24 worksheet file in the page provided by pressing **Ctrl+V**.

End of lab.

LAB 25
CONFIGURING SYSTEM RECOVERY OPTIONS

THIS LAB CONTAINS THE FOLLOWING EXERCISES AND ACTIVITIES:

Exercise 25.1 Creating and Reverting to a System Restore Point

Exercise 25.2 Using Windows Safe Mode

Exercise 25.3 Performing a File Restore from Backup

Lab Challenge Performing a PC Reset

BEFORE YOU BEGIN

The lab environment consists of student workstations connected to a local area network, along with a server that functions as the domain controller for a domain called adatum.com. The computers required for this lab are listed in Table 25-1.

Table 25-1
Computers Required for Lab 25

Computer	*Operating System*	*Computer Name*
Server	Windows Server 2012	SVR-DC-A
Client	Windows 8 Enterprise	WKSTN-MBR-B
Client	Windows 7 Enterprise	WKSTN-MBR-C

In addition to the computers, you will also need the software listed in Table 25-2 to complete Lab 25.

Table 25-2
Software Required for Lab 25

Software	***Location***
Lab 25 student worksheet	Lab25_worksheet.docx (provided by instructor)

Working with Lab Worksheets

Each lab in this manual requires that you answer questions, shoot screen shots, and perform other activities that you will document in a worksheet named for the lab, such as Lab25_worksheet.docx. You will find these worksheets on the book companion site. It is recommended that you use a USB flash drive to store your worksheets so you can submit them to your instructor for review. As you perform the exercises in each lab, open the appropriate worksheet file, type the required information, and then save the file to your flash drive.

SCENARIO

After completing this lab, you will be able to:

- Create and revert to a system restore point
- Boot Windows into Safe Mode
- Backup and restore files using Windows 7 Backup

Estimated lab time: 70 minutes

Exercise 25.1	Creating and Reverting to a System Restore Point
Overview	In this exercise, you will create a restore point that can be used to roll back the system files and programs to a previously saved restore point.
Mindset	Sometimes when you install or upgrade a program, Windows or the program does not run properly. If you have a restore point, you can recover from these problems by rolling back to the previous point.
Completion time	15 minutes

1. On **WKSTN-MBR-B**, log on using the **adatum\administrator** account and the **Pa$$w0rd** password.

2. Type **Control Panel** and then click the **Control Panel** icon.

3. In the *Search Control Panel* text box, type **Create a Restore point** and then press **Enter**. When the *Create a restore point* option is displayed, click **Create a restore point**.

Question 1	*Which drive is listed in the Protection Settings box?*

4. In the *System Properties* dialog box (see Figure 25-1), click **Configure**.

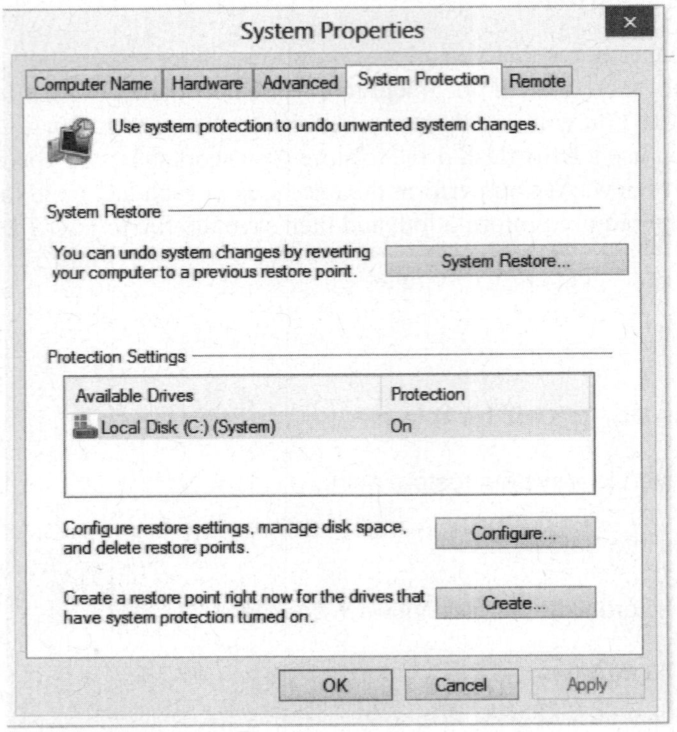

Figure 25-1
The *System Properties* page

5. When the *System Protection for Local Disk (C:)* dialog box opens, click to select **Turn on system protection**. Then slide *Max Usage:* to **10%**.

6. Click **OK** to close the *System Protection for Local Disk (C:)* dialog box.

7. To create a restore point, click **Create**.

8. In the *System Protection* dialog box, in the *Description* text box, type **Test** and then click **Create**.

9. When the restore point is created, take a screen shot of the *System Protection* dialog box by pressing **Alt+Prt Scr** and then paste it into your Lab 25 worksheet file in the page provided by pressing **Ctrl+V**.

10. Click **Close**.

11. In the *System Properties* dialog box, click **System Restore**.

12. When the *System Restore* Wizard opens, click **Next**.

13. Click the **Test** restore point that you just made and then click **Next**.

14. In the *Confirm your restore point* dialog box, click **Finish**.

15. When presented with a warning message indicating that system restore cannot be interrupted, click **Yes** to continue.

16. After WKSTN-MBR-B reboots, log on as **adatum\administrator** using the **Pa$$w0rd** password.

17. Click the **Desktop** tile.

18. The system restore is completed. Take a screen shot of the *System Restore* dialog box by pressing **Alt+Prt Scr** and then paste it into your Lab 25 worksheet file in the page provided by pressing **Ctrl+V**.

19. Click **Close** to close the *System Restore* dialog box.

End of exercise. Leave WKSTN-MBR-B running and logged in for the next exercise.

Exercise 25.2	Using Windows Safe Mode
Overview	In this exercise, you will boot to Safe Mode and look at the various tools that are available in Safe Mode that can be used to troubleshoot Windows.
Mindset	Safe Mode is a troubleshooting option used for Windows that launches Windows with basic files and drivers.
Completion time	20 minutes

1. Mouse over the lower-left corner of the desktop and right-click the **Start** screen thumbnail that appears there. Then, from the context menu that appears, click **Command Prompt (Admin)**.

2. At the command prompt, execute the following command:

   shutdown /r /o

3. When prompted to shut down the system, click **Close**. The system will shut down in less than a minute.

4. Click the **Troubleshoot** tile.

5. Click the **Advanced options** tile.

6. Click **Startup Settings**.

7. Select **Restart**.

8. When the *Startup Settings* options show (see Figure 25-2), press **4** on the keyboard.

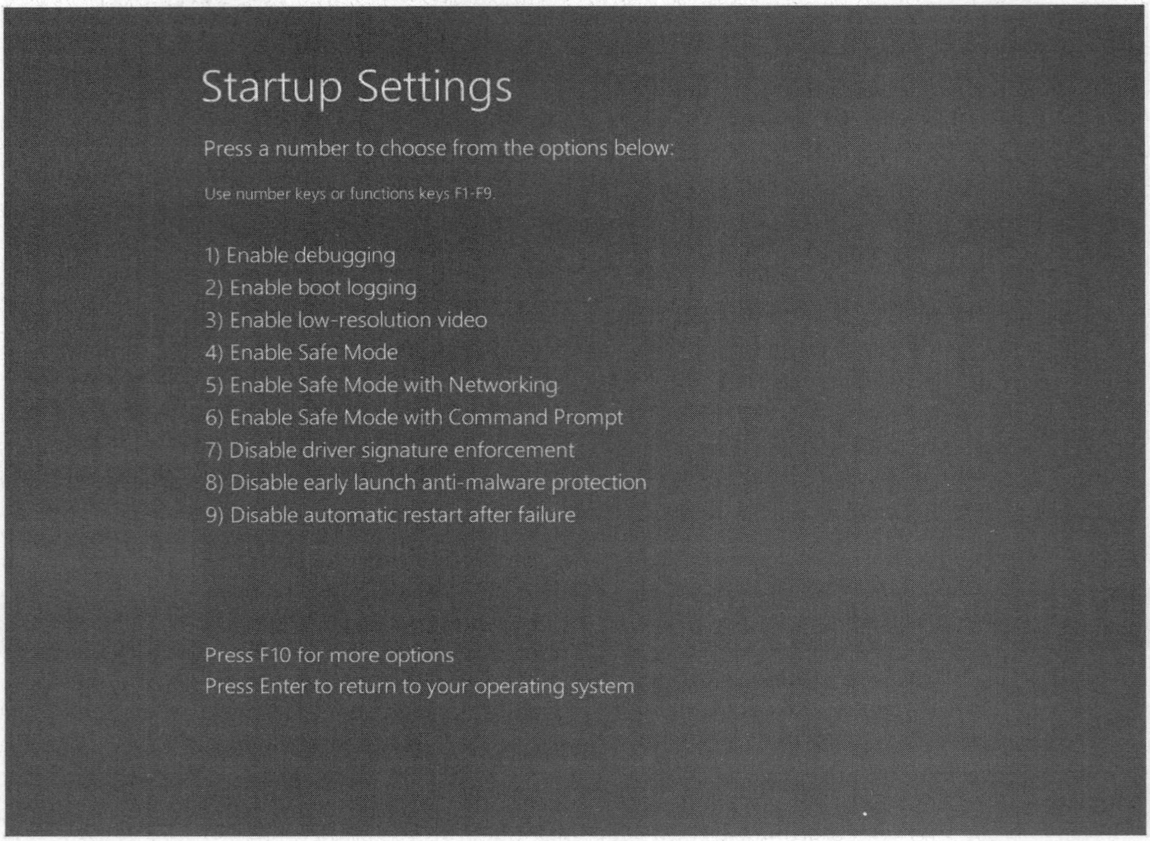

Figure 25-2
The *Startup Settings* page

9. After WKSTN-MBR-B boots, log in as **adatum\administrator** using the **Pa$$w0rd** password.

10. Close the **Windows Help and Support** window.

11. Mouse over the lower-left corner of the desktop and click the **Start** screen thumbnail that appears there. Then, on the *Start* page, type **msconfig** and then click the **msconfig** tile.

12. Take a screen shot of the *General* tab by pressing **Alt+Prt Scr** and then paste it into your Lab 25 worksheet file in the page provided by pressing **Ctrl+V**.

13. Click the **Boot** tab.

Question 2	*What is the boot entry that is shown?*

14. Click the **Services** tab.

Question 3	*How many services are running? (Click the Status column to sort the Running vs Stopped entries to make it easier to count the Running entries).*

15. Click to select **Hide all Microsoft services**.

Question 4	*How many non-Microsoft services do you have?*

16. Click **OK** to close the *System Configuration* window.

17. Mouse over the lower-left corner of the desktop and click the **Start** screen thumbnail that appears there. Then, on the screen, type **compmgmt.msc** and then click the **compmgmt tile**.

Question 5	*Which program was opened by typing compmgmt?*

18. Click **Event Viewer** > **Windows Logs** and then review the *System* log and the *Application* log. (If you were actually experiencing a problem, you would look for events that would help you troubleshoot the problem.)

19. Close the **Computer Management** console.

20. Use **File Explorer** to navigate to the **C:\Windows** folder and locate the **ntbtlog.txt** file.

21. Open the **ntbtlog.txt** file to view its contents.

22. Take a screen shot of the *ntbtlog* file by pressing **Alt+Prt Scr** and then paste it into your Lab 25 worksheet file in the page provided by pressing **Ctrl+V**.

23. Close the **ntbtlog.txt** file.

24. Move the mouse pointer to the bottom-right corner to display the Charms bar. Then click **Settings** > **Power** > **Restart** to restart the computer.

End of exercise.

Exercise 25.3	Performing a File Restore from Backup
Overview	In this exercise, you will back up some files and then restore one of those files using the Windows 7 Backup program.
Mindset	When you are having computer problems and all other troubleshooting efforts fail to reveal the issue, you can restore from a backup (assuming you took the precaution of taking a backup).
Completion time	25 minutes

1. On **SVR-DC-A**, log in using the **Adatum\administrator** account and the **Pa$$w0rd** password.
2. On the *Taskbar*, click **File Explorer**.
3. Create a **C:\Data** folder.
4. Right-click the **C:\Data** folder and choose **Properties**.
5. In the *Data Properties* dialog box, click the **Sharing** tab.
6. Click the **Advanced Sharing** button.
7. In the *Advanced Sharing* dialog box, click to select **Share this folder**.
8. Click the **Permissions** button.
9. Click to select **Allow Full Control Permission** for the *Everyone* group.
10. Click **OK** to close the *Permissions for Data* dialog box.
11. Click **OK** to close the *Advanced Sharing* dialog box.
12. Click **Close** to close the *Data Properties* dialog box.
13. Log into WKSTN-MBR-B as **contoso\administrator** using the **Pa$$w0rd** password. Click the **Desktop** tile.
14. Mouse over the lower-left corner of the desktop and right-click the **Start** screen thumbnail that appears there. Then, from the context menu that appears, click the **Control Panel** option.
15. In the *Search Control Panel* text box, type **Windows 7 File Recovery** and click **Windows 7 File Recovery** link. The Windows 7 File Recovery page appears (see Figure 25-3).

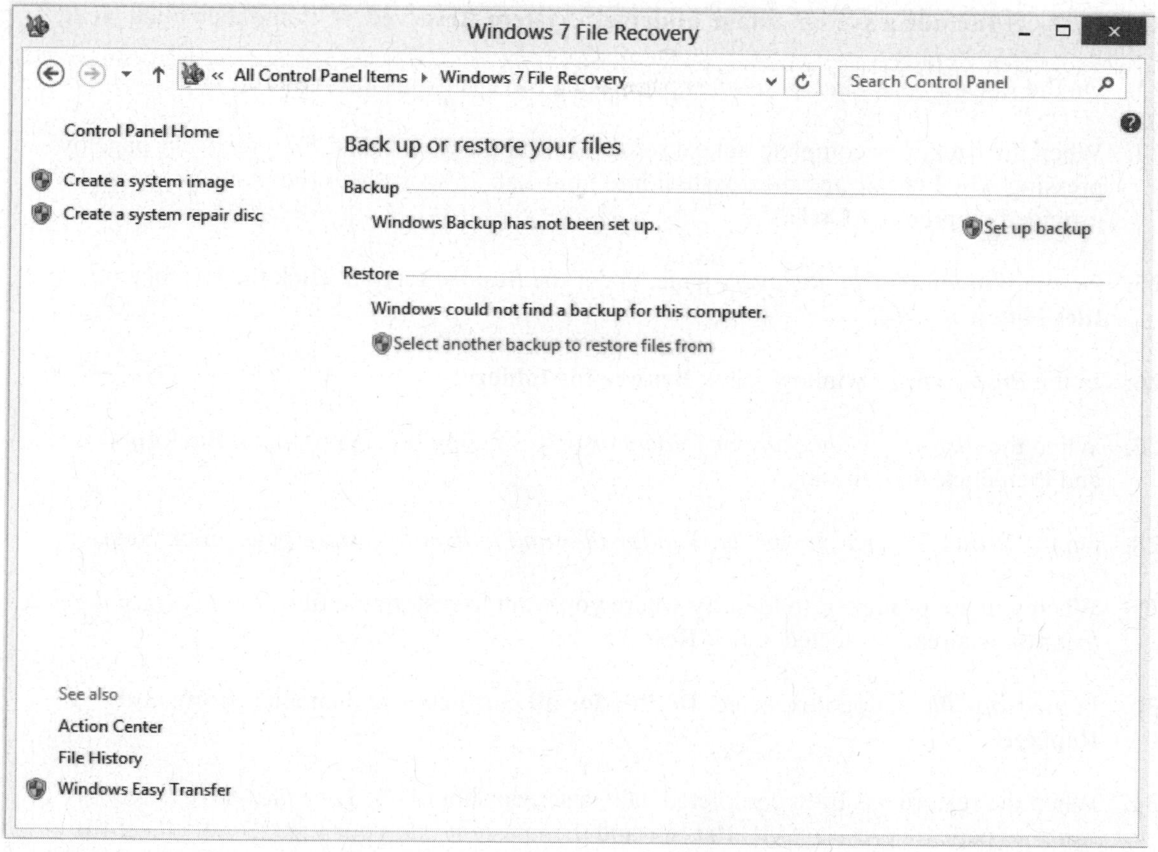

Figure 25-3
The *Windows 7 File Recovery* page

16. Click **Set up backup**.

17. On the *Set up backup* page, click **Save on a network**.

18. When the *Set up backup* page opens, ... In the *Network location* text box, type **\\svr-dc-a\data**.

19. In the *Username* text box, type **adatum\administrator**. In the *Password* text box, type **Pa$$w0rd**. Click **OK**.

20. On the *Set up backup* page, ensure **\\SVR-DC-A\data** is selected and then click **Next**.

21. On the *What do you want to back up?* page, select the **Let me choose** option and then click **Next**.

Question 6	*By default, which items are selected for backup?*

22. Deselect **Include a system image of drives: System Reserved, (C:)** and then click **Next**.

23. On the *Review your backup settings* page, click **Save settings and run backup**.

24. When the backup is complete, take a screen shot of the *Windows 7 File Recovery* page by pressing **Alt+Prt Scr** and then paste it into your Lab 25 worksheet file in the page provided by pressing **Ctrl+V**.

25. On the *Windows 7 File Recovery* page, under the *Restore* section, click the **Restore my files** button.

26. In the *Restore Files* window, click **Browse for folders**.

27. When the *Browse the backup for folders or drives* dialog box opens, click **Backup of C:** and then click **Add folder**.

28. On the *Browse or search your backup for files and folders to restore* page, click **Next**.

29. When you are prompted to identify where you want to restore the files, *In the original location* is already selected. Click **Restore**.

30. In the *Copy file* dialog box, select **Do this for all conflicts** and then click **Copy and Replace**.

31. When the restore has been completed, take a screen shot of the *Your files have been restored* page by pressing **Alt+Prt Scr** and then paste it into your Lab 25 worksheet file in the page provided by pressing **Ctrl+V**.

32. Click **Finish**.

33. Close **Windows 7 File Recovery**.

End of exercise. Leave Windows open for the next exercise.

Lab Challenge	Performing a PC Reset
Overview	In this exercise, you will demonstrate how to perform a PC reset.
Mindset	A PC reset allows you reset the computer to its factory settings, removing all of your personal files and apps. A PC refresh allows you to reset the computer without affecting your files.
Completion time	10 minutes

During this exercise, you will specify the steps to perform a PC reset. This exercise is a written exercise.

End of lab.

LAB 26
CONFIGURING FILE RECOVERY OPTIONS

THIS LAB CONTAINS THE FOLLOWING EXERCISES AND ACTIVITIES:

Exercise 26.1 Using File History

Lab Challenge Configuring the Advanced Settings of File History

BEFORE YOU BEGIN

The lab environment consists of student workstations connected to a local area network, along with a server that functions as the domain controller for a domain called adatum.com. The computers required for this lab are listed in Table 26-1.

Table 26-1
Computers required for Lab 26

Computer	*Operating System*	*Computer Name*
Server	Windows Server 2012	SVR-DC-A
Client	Windows 8 Enterprise	WKSTN-MBR-B

In addition to the computers, you will also need the software listed in Table 26-2 to complete Lab 26.

Table 26-2
Software Required for Lab 26

Software	*Location*
Lab 26 student worksheet	Lab26_worksheet.docx (provided by instructor)

Working with Lab Worksheets

Each lab in this manual requires that you answer questions, shoot screen shots, and perform other activities that you will document in a worksheet named for the lab, such as Lab26_worksheet.docx. You will find these worksheets on the book companion site. It is recommended that you use a USB flash drive to store your worksheets so you can submit them to your instructor for review. As you perform the exercises in each lab, open the appropriate worksheet file, type the required information, and then save the file to your flash drive.

SCENARIO

After completing this lab, you will be able to:

- Restore a file that is saved in File History
- Configure the advanced settings of File History

Estimated lab time: 30 minutes

Exercise 26.1	Using File History
Overview	In this exercise, you will restore a file that is saved in File History.
Mindset	File History is an alternative to Windows 7 File Recovery. It allows for files backed up on previous versions of Windows to be recovered.
Completion time	20 minutes

1. On **WKSTN-MBR-B**, log on using the **adatum\administrator** account and the **Pa$$w0rd** password. Click the **Desktop** tile.
2. Right-click the **Desktop** and choose **New > Text Document**. Name the document **Test**.
3. Mouse over the lower-left corner of the desktop and right-click the **Start** screen thumbnail that appears there. Then, from the context menu that appears, click the **Control Panel** icon.
4. Click **System and Security** and then click **File History**.

Question 1	*According to what's shown on-screen, which feature must be disabled before you can use File History?*

5. Click **Configure Windows 7 Backup**.
6. On the *Windows 7 File Recovery* page, click **Turn off schedule**.

7. On the *Windows 7 File Recovery* page, click the back arrow.

8. On the *File History* page (see Figure 26-1), click **Use network location.**

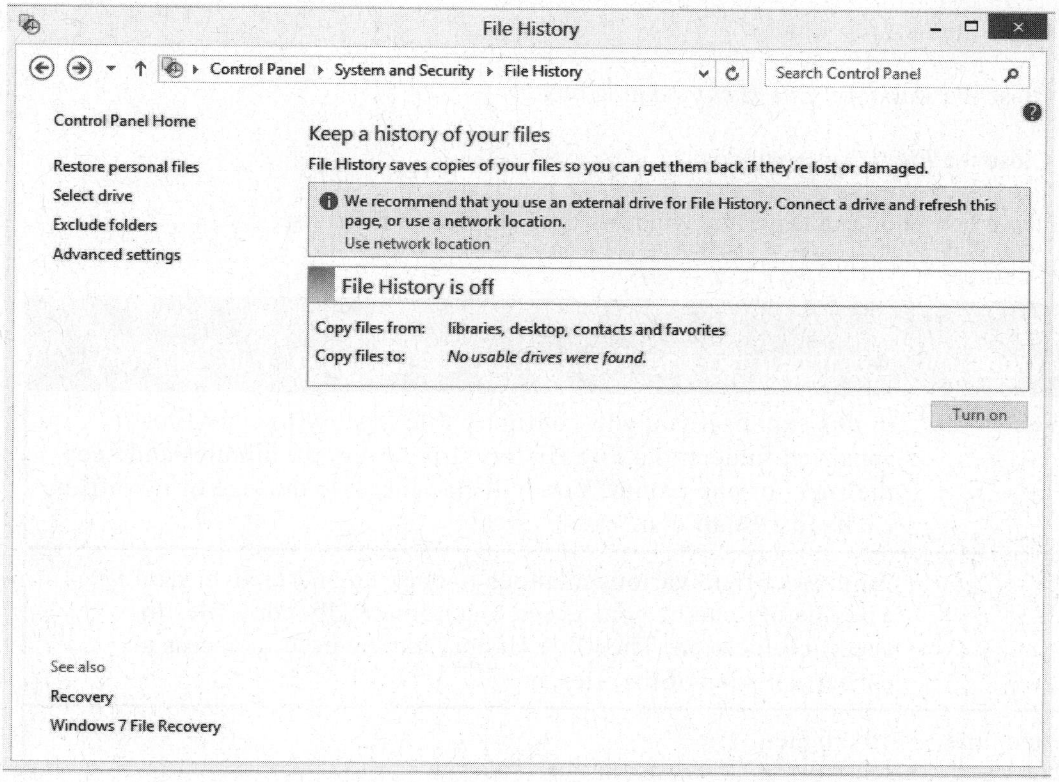

Figure 26-1
The *File History* page

9. On the *Select Drive* page, click **Add network location.**

10. In the *Select Folder* dialog box, in the *Folder* text box, type **\\SVR-DC-A\Data** and then click **Select Folder**.

11. On the *Select Drive* page, click **OK**.

12. On the *File History* page, click **Turn on**.

13. Click **Run now**.

14. Take a screen shot of the *File History* window by pressing **Alt+Prt Scr** and then paste it into your Lab 26 worksheet file in the page provided by pressing **Ctrl+V**.

15. In the left pane, click **Restore personal files**.

16. On the *Home - File History* window, double-click **Desktop**.

17. Click **Test** and then click the **Restore to original location** button (green button) at the bottom of the window.

18. In the *Replace or Skip Files* dialog box, click **Replace this file in the destination**.

19. **Close** the *Desktop* window.

20. **Close** the *Desktop - File History* dialog box.

21. **Close** the *File History* window.

End of exercise. You can leave any windows open for the next exercise.

Lab Challenge	Configuring the Advanced Settings of File History
Overview	In this exercise, you will configure File History to copy files in specified folders to a File History drive every 30 minutes and keep the files for one month. You will also increase the size of the offline cache to 10% of disk space.
Mindset	Windows offers various methods to back up and recover data files. File History can be configured to automatically copy files to a specified location. Then File History can be used to access an earlier versions of the files.
Completion time	10 minutes

To complete this challenge, you must have a virtual machine on your computer running Windows 8. You will write out the procedure to configure the Advanced Settings of File History. Then you will take a snapshot of the *File History Advanced Settings* page by pressing **Alt+Prt Scr** and then paste the resulting image into the Lab 26 worksheet file in the page provided by pressing **Ctrl+V**.

End of lab.